A Light Shines in Central Asia

A Journey into the Tibetan Buddhist World

Thomas Hale

William Carey Library
Pasadena, California

Cover design by *M. Sequeira*

ISBN 0-87808-350-2

Published by:
William Carey Library
P.O. Box 40129
Pasadena, CA 91114

Author's Home Mission:
InterServe (International Service Fellowship)
Box 418
Upper Darby, PA 19802

Library of Congress Cataloging-in-Publication Data

Hale, Thomas, 1937-
    A light shines in central Asia : a journey into the Tibetan
Buddhist world / by Thomas Hale.
        p. cm.
        ISBN 0-87808-350-2 (alk. paper)
    1. Missions--Asia, Central--History--20th Century. 2. Christian
converts from Buddhism--Biography. I. Title.
    BV3220 .H35 1999
    266'.00958--dc21   99-044970

---

 6 5 4 3 2 1
04 03 02 01 00

CONTENTS

INTRODUCTION

The term "Tibetan Buddhist world" is used in this book to designate all those people who follow the particular branch of Buddhist tradition known as Tibetan Buddhism. These Tibetan Buddhists are not limited to Tibet proper, but they comprise a number of different nationalities and ethnic groups located throughout Central Asia, almost all of them unreached with the gospel of Christ. I have written this book to highlight the needs of these Tibetan Buddhist peoples, and to do this, I propose to take the reader on a journey with me into their world.

Thus this book is not a treatise on Tibetan Buddhism per se. Rather it consists of the stories of modern-day Christians who are working in various parts of the Tibetan Buddhist world, and of Tibetan Buddhists themselves who have come to Christ and are now ministering among their own people. Though in most cases names and biographical details have been altered to protect people's identity, the stories are true in essence and their spiritual significance remains unaltered.

The Tibetan Buddhist peoples have over the centuries been one of the groups most resistant to the gospel of Christ. Since the seventh century A.D., first the Nestorian Christians, later Catholics, and finally Protestants have attempted to bring the gospel to the Tibetan Buddhist world, but in almost every case they have met with a signal lack of success. Only in recent years have notable advances been made, mainly in Nepal and in Mongolia. But increasingly the worldwide Christian community is focusing on the vast, unreached Tibetan Buddhist areas of Central Asia, and inroads are beginning to be made. It is hoped that this book will inspire others to join those already working in this difficult harvest field. Twenty million Tibetan Buddhists, spread out from Siberia in the north to India and Nepal in the south, have not yet had the claims of Christ presented to them in a relevant and understandable way. " . . . how can they hear without someone preaching to them?" (Rom. 10:14). "Ask the Lord of the harvest, therefore, to send out workers into his harvest field" (Matt. 9:38).

Tibetan Buddhism traces its origin back to the Buddha, who was born in Nepal approximately six hundred years before Christ. But the Buddha himself based his teachings on a much older tradition, Hinduism; indeed, the Buddha did not set out so much to establish a new religion as to reform an old one. Only as the Buddha's followers carried his teaching beyond present-day India did Buddhism become fully established as a religion distinct from Hinduism. Indeed, within India itself, the Buddha's influence progressively waned, until today there are very few adherents of Buddhism among India's native-born population.

The ancient tradition on which the Buddha based his teaching was brought to India in the second millennium before Christ by Aryan invaders from the northwest. Their oldest scriptures are the Vedas, which have been elaborated and amplified by religious teachers down through the centuries, resulting in what we today know as Hinduism.

The ancient tradition of Vedaism consisted of three key elements, which continue to influence the world view of Hindus and Buddhists to the present day. The first element is the belief in a universal and impersonal being (called Atman or Brahman), which is the source of all reality.

The second element is the belief that everything that exists is simply part of this underlying reality, or Atman. Atman is the ground of existence for everything; thus everything is essentially one. This belief is called monism. According to monism, there is no essential difference between a person, a star, or a bug. Neither is there any essential difference between the concepts of good and evil, or between love and hate. All are just part of the same underlying reality, Atman.

The third element is the belief that what our senses tell us is merely an illusion. The idea that a person is a separate and unique entity is an illusion, because we are all one, a part of Atman. The world we experience around us is an illusion, a dream from which we cannot wake up. We don't know that it's only a dream, and this ignorance is the root of our problem. The way to "wake up" is through "enlightenment."

These three elements sound like philosophical abstractions, but they have practical ramifications in the lives of millions of Hindus and

Buddhists today. For example, the notion that we as individuals have no separate existence undermines the value of human life and personhood. There can be no personal life after death; we merely merge again into the Atman.

Furthermore, if everything around us is an illusion, then there is no point in overcoming adversity, because adversity is an illusion. This idea leads to fatalism, which is a prominent part of Hindu and Buddhist thought. This fatalism is one reason why predominantly Hindu and Buddhist societies remain backward and mired in poverty. For example, why worry about germs if they don't really exist? The effect of such thinking on people's health is obvious.

As Vedaism developed over the ensuing centuries, other ideas were added to it. One of these was the idea of rebirth, according to which an impersonal "life force" in each of us passes on at our death to be reborn in another being. This would mean that every living person has had thousands of previous lives, some lived as humans, but most lived as animals, ghosts, or hell-beings. Which life one has depends on another idea that has strongly influenced both Hinduism and Buddhism, the idea of "karma."

Karma is more than just blind fate. It means that for every action there is a consequence, and that that consequence will carry over into one's next life. Good actions result in merit; bad actions result in demerit. The status of a person's present life depends on the relative amounts of merit and demerit accumulated during one's previous lives. According to this idea, if adversity strikes someone, it is that person's own fault; he or she is simply reaping the reward of his or her previous life. Likewise, if one is rich or successful, it is the result of virtuous actions in that person's previous lives.

The doctrines of rebirth and karma provide the greatest motivating force in Hinduism and Buddhism today. The practical religious life of most Hindus and Buddhists centers on the gaining of merit in order to ensure a better situation in one's next life. In order to gain merit, Hindus and Buddhists carefully observe all the prescribed rituals and rules laid down by their religious leaders, they bring offerings to their deities, they give alms and do many other good works—all in the effort to improve their lot in the next life.

As the centuries passed, some of the early Hindu religious leaders began to devise ways to shortcut this tedious progression of rebirths. They turned to various austerities as a means of gaining extra merit, and some even dreamed of breaking out of the cycle of rebirth altogether. One such leader was Siddhartha Gautama, who became known as the Buddha, or "enlightened one."

Little is known with certainty concerning the Buddha's life and work. It was not until three hundred years after his death that the story of the Buddha's life was written down, and by that time the facts had become embellished with many myths and legends. (This is in contrast to the facts of Jesus' life, which were written down by His contemporaries within a few decades of His death.)

The Buddha accepted the basic presuppositions of Hinduism: namely, that man's progress to an ever higher state could only be realized through self-effort and that the visible world and everything associated with it was an illusion. There was no place in his thought for either a personal God or even for man's individual personhood. And he taught that the only way man could escape from suffering and rebirth was by shattering the illusion of self through inner realization or enlightenment.

The Buddha summarized his teaching in what has become known as the "Four Noble Truths": (1) life is characterized by suffering; (2) suffering arises from desire; (3) suffering is overcome by extinguishing desire, which results in a state called "nirvana," or literally, "extinction"; and (4) desire can be extinguished by following the "eightfold path." The eightfold path itself can be summarized as right views, right intention, right speech, right action, right livelihood, right effort, right mindfulness, and right concentration.

The Buddha thus offered the Hindus of North India a truly new path, a path with no caste system, no rituals, no expensive priests, no gods—only self-reliance and self-effort. By turning to self, one could overcome the illusion of self and eliminate suffering.

It is popular today to focus on the similarities between Buddhism and Christianity, even to the point of saying that they are two equally valid paths to the same truth. But any similarities between Buddhism and Christianity are strictly superficial. At root, the two systems are polar opposites. As a Christian, I must clearly state that Buddhism is fundamentally false, and this for two main reasons: first, it denies the existence of a personal God; and second, it claims that man can be saved by his own effort. This is Satan's ultimate deception, and so it has been from the beginning.

In the second century before Christ, Buddhism divided into two great schools: one, the "Mahayana" school, which spread northward into China, Korea and Japan; and two, the "Hinayana" school, which spread into Southeast Asia. The Hinayana school remained truer to the original teachings of the Buddha, whereas the Mahayana school added many elements that the Buddha never taught.

Several things distinguished Mahayana Buddhism, out of which Tibetan Buddhism was eventually to emerge. First was the teaching that one can gain enlightenment or salvation in a single lifetime, rather than the thousands of lifetimes required under classical Buddhism. This concept transformed Buddhism from being a religion of a few elite monks to a religion accessible to the masses. Anyone could now become a monk and save himself, and in one lifetime.

Second, because the path to nirvana had been so drastically shortened, some Buddhists were led to delay their entrance into nirvana and instead help others on their path to liberation. Those who did this became known as "Bodhisattvas." Anyone could thus become a Bodhisattva and save not only himself but others as well.

In time, many Bodhisattvas came to be regarded almost as gods, each with his own mythology. Thus a whole spiritual world was built up, which became as complex as the Hindu pantheon from which the Buddha had sought to free himself and his followers.

As Mahayana Buddhism spread northward, it encountered the indigenous religions of the people of Central Asia and China, religions which were essentially shamanistic and animistic. Instead of replacing these indigenous beliefs, Mahayana Buddhism adopted many of them, incorporating elements of magic, sorcery, tantric rituals, and blood sacrifice. In the process, Mahayana Buddhism was transformed into a religion of spirits, demons and sorcerers; and the shamans, or witch doctors, became its priests. This is the form of Tibetan Buddhism practiced by most people throughout Central Asia today.

In fairness, it must be pointed out that the "folk-Buddhism" practiced by the masses in Asia is quite different from the elite and scholarly Buddhism practiced by the monks in their monasteries and now being taught in intellectual centers throughout the West. Some of the more extreme shamanistic practices would indeed be frowned upon in these scholarly circles. Nonetheless, the fact remains that today's Tibetan Buddhism has arisen from a merging of Mahayana Buddhism and shamanism, and the result is a religion quite distinct from the teachings of the Buddha himself.

As Marku Tsering writes in his book, *Sharing Christ in the Tibetan Buddhist World*, there are ten features common to all Tibetan Buddhist cultures that are important to keep in mind when Christians witness to Tibetan Buddhists.

The ten features are: (1) an unquestioning faith, (2) a need for merit, (3) an ideal of detachment, (4) a lively folk religion, (5) an ideal of nonviolence, (6) a system of offerings, (7) Tibetan Buddhism as a national identity, (8) Tibetan language, (9) religious specialists, and (10) Tibetan art and architecture.

Tibetan Buddhists have unquestioning faith in their religious leaders, or lamas, and in the teaching of these lamas. Their belief system is self-contained; it purports to answer all of life's questions. Hence Tibetan Buddhists feel no need to go outside their own religious system to find answers to their questions.

The Tibetan Buddhist's chief practical goal in life is to accumulate religious merit. The Buddha's original system of merit and demerit operated mechanically, impersonally. Sin was a personal matter that affected only the sinner. But in Tibetan Buddhism, elaborate means of gaining extra merit have been devised, such as special ceremonies and rituals, magic spells, and worship of Bodhisattvas and other religious figures. The lamas, in particular, are able to influence how much merit one receives; and hence, like the Catholic priests in medieval times, they exert great power over the people.

An eyewitness in Bhutan once recorded a remarkable example of just how powerful the lamas can be. Bhutan's chief lama was planning a trip and needed a vehicle. So he coopted a bright maroon Land Rover that had been donated by a Norwegian mission to Bhutan's main government hospital. As the lama proceeded on his journey, he would bless the people along the roadside by touching them lightly with a long stick topped with a tuft of feathers. The blessing of such a high lama is believed to produce thousands of times more merit than a mere good deed or the blessing of an ordinary lama. So, as the bright maroon vehicle crept slowly through the crowds, hundreds of just-blessed devotees could be seen running ahead of the vehicle to get in line for a second blessing from the lama's feathered stick—and a third, and a fourth. This lama is said to be as powerful as the king of Bhutan—and no wonder, with so much merit flowing from the tip of his stick!

Since "making merit" is so important and so time consuming, it is not surprising that Tibetan Buddhists have developed an apparatus to assist them—the prayer wheel, the ultimate merit-making machine. A single prayer can be written thousands of times on a roll of paper, and each time the prayer wheel is turned, merit is accrued as if each of the prayers had been uttered separately. Some of the larger prayer wheels are rotated by water power, or even by electricity.

For most Tibetan Buddhists, the pursuit of merit has led them to place greater reliance on outward form and ritual than on inward purity. In addition, their everyday religious life is strongly influenced by shamanistic practices; occultism is widespread. Christians working among Tibetan Buddhist people must be aware of factors such as these, if they are to truly understand the spiritual forces arrayed against them.

One cannot win over Tibetan Buddhists by theoretical argument, or by radio or literature alone. Tibetan Buddhists must have a chance to see Christ's people, Christ's witnesses, living and working among them; they will only come to know Christ as they see Him in the lives of His followers. Thus Christ places a great responsibility on those He calls to minister in the Tibetan Buddhist world; they need to represent Him wisely and effectively. To do this they need, above all, the power and the filling of the Holy Spirit.

There are a number of special cautions which those called to Tibetan Buddhist work must heed. Some of these are common to all missionary work. First and foremost is the need for the Christian to live a life that the Buddhist will regard as holy. The worker must take care not to give unnecessary offense. For example, the Christian must show respect not only to the Tibetan Buddhists themselves but also to their sacred texts and traditions. There is no place for arrogance or scoffing. Christians must adopt a life style comparable to the life style of those they work among. They should leave at home many of their Western gadgets and appliances; these will merely convince the Buddhist that Christians are worldly and unspiritual.

Beyond outward customs and behavior, the Christian must learn to empathize and identify with the people he is called to serve. He must learn to see the world as they see it. Only then will he be able to come alongside them as an equal and share with them as a friend. Only in this way will he be able to discern their point of spiritual need and lead them to the One who can meet that need.

It is obvious that to work among Tibetan Buddhists effectively, one must learn their language. There is no shortcut around this. But even when one has become fluent, difficulties remain. Tibetan Buddhists and Christians may use the same word to describe utterly opposing concepts. For example, both speak of God, but the Christian sees Him as a loving heavenly Father, while the Tibetan Buddhist thinks only of an impersonal abstract being. Both speak of prayer, but one means talking with the Father and the other means spinning a prayer wheel. Both use the word "incarnation"; but Christians think of the one true incarnation, Jesus, fully divine and fully human. Buddhists consider an incarnation to be a person who somehow emanates from a teacher or deity. There are millions of such incarnations in Tibetan Buddhism, but they are not divine, only human.

Finally, both Christians and Tibetan Buddhists talk about rebirth and eternal life, but how far apart their meanings are! For the Christian, rebirth comes through the Holy Spirit; for the Buddhist, rebirth is simply the next life. The Buddhist sees eternal life as an endless succession of rebirths from which he longs to escape. The Christian believes that eternal life is joyful, tearless, everlasting fellowship with God, the central element of our salvation.

Jesus has a message for the Tibetan Buddhists, a message of forgiveness, of love, of hope. They need the chance to hear His message. Who will go for Him? Who will say, "Here am I, Lord; send me"?

PREFACE

"I'm suffering from constipation," said the Rinpoche, or chief lama. This news was transmitted by the Rinpoche's interpreter from Tibetan into Nepali, and hence through our Nepali interpreter into English.

This was our first meeting with a Tibetan Buddhist. The year was 1970. My wife Cynthia and I were brand new medical missionaries to the kingdom of Nepal, and within two weeks of arriving in the country we had been asked to conduct a weekly medical clinic in a Tibetan Buddhist monastery just outside Kathmandu. The regular doctor, Bethel Fleming, one of the founders of the United Mission to Nepal under which we worked, was out of the country, and we had been asked to take her place running the clinic.

This particular monastery was perched on a high hill overlooking Kathmandu, part of a famous Buddhist temple complex called Swayambhunath. About twenty monks lived there; they were refugees from Tibet, having fled to Nepal when the Chinese Communists took over their land in 1959. Our weekly clinic began at two o'clock, and had to be over by four, as that was when afternoon vespers began. After examining the Rinpoche and prescribing some medicine, we examined the remaining monks, most of whom had the same malady their leader was suffering from. After the clinic we would usually be invited to the Rinpoche's private apartment for tea. This was like no tea we had ever drank. It was a lukewarm mixture of bitter tea, salt, and yak butter; it was the most unpleasant concoction I had ever tasted. Cynthia generally put a good face on it, however, which you have to do when you venture into other people's culture.

At four the vespers would start. Six monks provided the music. Two monks blew into long, elaborately carved horns. Another beat a huge drum. One rotund monk sat apart at the base of a twelve-foot-high statue of the Buddha, clanging a pair of cymbals. The music was eerie, foreboding and, after a time, monotonous. Other monks sat around and chanted to the music. The hall was dimly lit with butter lamps and the air was heavy with incense.

This was our first taste of Tibetan Buddhism, a religion of twenty million people spread out from the semitropical jungles of Nepal and India to the arctic forests of Siberia. These people are the least reached of all the world's people, and they have the fewest Christian witnesses working among them. The whole vast region of Central Asia, stretching for thousands of miles in all directions, is like a great wasteland, forgotten and untouched. But it will not remain so for long. The worldwide church is waking up, and workers are just now beginning to enter that little-known region. This book will provide a glimpse of what God is doing among the Tibetan Buddhist peoples today, and it will introduce the reader to a few of God's choice servants, both foreign and national, whom God is using to build His kingdom throughout Central Asia.

But first back to Swayambhunath. Leaving the moaning of the horns and the echoes of the cymbals and drums behind, we needed to get down the hill, past a hundred monkeys poised to snatch camera or handbag, and back to the mission guest house in time for supper, where Lilly, the Swiss hostess, would be waiting to serve up some pungent sausage meat that gave every indication it had traveled overland from Switzerland in the hot summer sun. But not to worry; it would take away the taste of the Tibetan tea. As one Asian restaurant advertised: "Our food will leave you with an everlasting aftertaste." That restaurant had nothing on Lilly's sausage.

Our batch of new missionaries lived for five months at the mission guest house under Lilly's tutelage. Then we all dispersed to the various projects to which we had been assigned. Cynthia and I went out to a mission hospital eighty miles northwest of Kathmandu as a crow flies. But we couldn't get there like a crow does; we had to take a bus for six to ten hours (depending on the condition of the road and the condition of the bus) and then walk fifteen miles up a mountain to reach the hospital. Why would you build a hospital near the top of a mountain? you ask. Well, in the Himalayan foothills of Nepal the people are evenly distributed in the valleys and on the mountains, so it didn't matter where we put the hospital: it would be equally accessible to all. Indeed, having the hospital at the top of a mountain worked in our favor: patients felt weak and weary climbing up the mountain and felt strong and vigorous walking down, a change we imagined they might attribute in some measure to our treatment.

Cynthia and I worked for twelve years at that hospital, during which time we met many Nepalis of Tibetan Buddhist background. Roughly a quarter of Nepal's 23 million people practice some form of Tibetan Buddhism. One of the first of these Buddhists to become a Christian in our area was a young man named Prem.

PREM'S STORY

CHAPTER ONE

At ten o'clock the moon was just appearing above the eastern ridge; the village lay silent. Prem Gurung quietly put aside his blanket, walked softly across the tiny room, paused a moment at the doorway to make sure his parents were asleep, and stepped out into the moonlight. He headed up the path leading to the high ridge behind the village. Prem made his way quickly along the well-lit path; he had waited for such a night as this, with full moon and clear sky, to make his escape. The ridge top stood two thousand feet above the village. Once on top the way would be easier, mostly downhill for many miles; then a steep descent, two thousand feet down, and then an equal climb back up to the village of Amp Pipal, his journey's end. If he hurried, and if no clouds blew up to hide the moon, he'd be able to reach Amp Pipal by dawn. By the time his parents had woken up, he'd be safely out of their reach. They wouldn't even know where to look for him.

Prem Gurung was eleven. It was 1958, and a new school had recently opened in Amp Pipal, started, it was said, by an "Americani" schoolteacher. Since there had never been such a thing as a school before in that part of the district, its opening created a great stir among the populace. Most people had little notion of what a school was all about, but they were quite sure, nonetheless, that they wanted to send their sons there to learn how to read, write, and get a big government job in the city. That's what schools were for in India, some said, and there was no reason to think that this school would be any different.

Jonathan Lindell, the school's founder and the first missionary to come to Amp Pipal, had far different intentions for the school. His vision was to train young Nepalis to be good citizens right in their own communities, not to encourage them to go off and get high-paying jobs somewhere else. With this in mind he planned to offer classes up to fifth grade and no higher: a fifth-grade education would not be enough to qualify for a job in the city.

People's expectations have a way of overcoming one's best-laid plans, and in the case of the Amp Pipal mission school the community was not content to limit their school to five classes. During the first few years, of course, the issue never arose, seeing there were no fifth-grade students to worry about. But as the school's fame grew in those first few years, spreading even to Prem's village a night's walk away, so grew the aspirations of the students and their parents; so that by the time the first fifth-grade class was ready to "graduate," the community had raised such an outcry that Mr. Lindell felt obliged to add on three more grades. The villagers were happy; the clinking coins of Kathmandu salaries were already sounding in their ears.

Prem had visited Amp Pipal once before when an older friend had taken him to see the new school. They had stayed overnight at the home of a village woman who, for a small fee, let students board at her house. Prem at once saw the possibilities that an education might open up for him; not that these possibilities took distinct shape in his imagination, but rather they appeared as a rosy glow on the horizon beckoning him to a life beyond the narrow confines of his little valley, a life in the great world outside, of which he knew almost nothing. When Prem got back home and saw with newly widened eyes the dead-end prospects his village offered, he went to his father and asked if he might enroll in the new school.

Prem's father looked at his only son and asked, "If you go to school, who will help me farm the land? Who will help look after the animals?"

Prem's family were subsistence farmers. Prem and his sisters spent most of their time helping on the tiny farm. Play was unknown to them. The family could raise enough food on their land to last them, on average, eight months of the year—ten months in a good year, six months in a bad one. On the off months, Prem's father would try to find odd jobs carrying loads or helping other people build their houses. When work was scarce, the family cut back to eating one meal a day. Poverty constricted their lives, and like so many of their fellow villagers, they simply resigned themselves to their lot and plodded onwards. Except for Prem.

The father refused to grant Prem's request to go to school, saying he was needed at home. The boy absorbed this blow to his hopes with seeming equanimity, but inwardly he rebelled against his father's decision. For Prem, school was more than a dream; it was a pathway to freedom, freedom from endless labor, freedom from poverty. From that day on he began to plan his escape. And now the moment had arrived.

Prem stepped gently from the porch down onto the courtyard in front of his house. Once out the gate and onto the main trail heading to the top of the ridge, he would feel safer. For now, though, he wished the moon was not so bright. Hearing a footstep behind him he looked quickly back, expecting to see his father coming out of the house; but he saw nothing. He walked quickly across the courtyard. Clang! He clattered into some cooking pots, which had been left outside after the evening meal. Big footsteps now. Rustling, creaking, the house seemed to come alive; shutters opened, doors banged.

Prem ran, stumbled into a ditch at the edge of the courtyard, and lay without moving. He was hidden from the big eye of the moon. He listened. The rustling and creaking subsided, and then came a loud snort. It was only the buffalo in its stall, alarmed by the clang of the pots.

Prem got up and once more looked back. The house looked blank and still. Prem thought of his parents and sisters, and felt a pang of heartsickness, even of remorse. He respected his father and loved his mother. But he resolutely turned toward the gate. For too many weeks he had been planning this night, eagerly looking ahead to this, his hour of freedom. There was no turning back.

Out the gate and free at last. He ran up the path until he was out of breath. No sound now, only the crickets, the buzzing *jhankri kira*, and his own pounding heart. The hoot of a scops owl startled him. Then quiet again.

He pushed on. A twig snapped under his foot, but the sound seemed to come from the thicket to his right. In his fright he thought of tigers stalking him, or robbers. He ran again, but when he turned and looked back there was nothing. Only the leaves rustling in the breeze, and the bamboo swaying and creaking above his head.

The path entered a forest, and walking became more difficult. Prem stubbed his bare toes against roots and rocks invisible in the shadows of the trees. It grew darker. Prem remembered stories he had heard about the spirits of dead people that came out in the forest at night.

They were said to wait at forks in the road and, when a traveler passed by, to jump out and seize him. People were known to have gone into the jungle at night and never come out. A friend of Prem's once told of an uncle who had actually seen one of these ghosts. They only attacked lone travelers—Prem remembered that; you were safe if you had a companion. He walked faster.

Every forest sound began to assume a sinister life of its own. The trail now ascended steeply, but still Prem hurried on. Gone were thoughts of father, mother, sisters; in their place were ghosts, chasing, racing through his imagination. A crashing in the underbrush to his left set Prem's heart skipping, as a jackal leapt across the path in front of him and scurried into the woods. Then, a few minutes later, he was out of the woods and onto the open moonlit terraces. In an instant he felt brave and confident again, glad once more to be on his way to the new mission school in Amp Pipal.

Early next morning after eight hours of weary trudging, slipping, and stumbling, Prem arrived in Amp Pipal. His arms were scratched, his knees scuffed. As he walked timidly through the sleepy bazaar, he saw standing in the doorway of her house the same pleasant-looking woman with whom he had stayed overnight the time before. Going up to her he said, "I've come to study in the new school. Do you know where I can stay? I have no place to live."

The woman inquired where he was from and why he had come all that way alone at night, and when she had satisfied herself that his story was true, she told him he could board at her house. She wasn't looking for money; she wasn't thinking of the household chores he might do for her—though of course he would do some. But she, too, had been a waif at one time, and her heart went out to him in sympathy. Besides, she was a naturally hospitable person, as are most Nepalis. Twelve years later, Cynthia and I would get to know this same woman well, for she would become our cook.

The two momentous steps of reaching Amp Pipal and finding a place to stay had been taken. The third step was an easy matter: to obtain a place in the school and begin studying—even though, when Prem arrived, classes had already been running a month. With the barest questioning—he was staying with an aunt, Prem said—he was admitted to the school; perhaps it was his bright and eager manner that gained him entrance. Whatever it was, he fully rewarded the expectations of his teachers. He quickly caught up with the rest of his class and went on to become a favorite with master and student alike. And when his family discovered where he was several weeks later, Prem was well-established as a bona fide scholar in the Amp Pipal mission school. It was his mother who came for him; but after two days of recrimination, defiance, and tears, she was sent away empty. Prem's father then vowed he'd bring the boy home again, but as he was about to set out to fetch him, he began to have second thoughts. Maybe an educated son just might be of greater value than a farmhand after all. In the end, the father let him stay.

Prem did not remain in school for long. Many of his fellow students continued their schooling and went on to the mission high school, a two-hour walk down the mountain, and from there on to college in Kathmandu. Many have since assumed important positions in their fields, and not a few have become leaders in Nepal's rapidly growing church. But such was not to be Prem's story. Toward the end of his first year in school, word came that his father had become ill and that Prem was urgently needed to help at home. Being the only son, it fell to him by Nepali custom to care for his parents and work on the family farm. So reluctantly he said good-bye to his teachers and his classmates and returned to his village. There some time later his father died, and Prem gave up all hope of returning to the mission school. However, the memory of his time at school remained with Prem, and the contact with his missionary teachers made a lasting impression upon him. He had gained a glimpse of a larger outside world, and had learned of a God who came to earth to heal and save. He had also learned to read.

Some years later Prem married a girl from his village named Laxmi, and they settled into the family home. Unlike many Nepali husbands whose marriages are arranged by their parents for purely economic and social reasons, Prem had a deep affection for his wife from the beginning. Thus it was all the more distressing to him when a couple of years later Laxmi became ill with tuberculosis. Prem's relatives and village friends insisted she be taken to the local shaman, or witch doctor, but after months of sacrificing chickens and submitting to various spells and other treatments, she had become worse. Her body burned with fever; her coughing at night kept both her and Prem from sleep. Like an uprooted flower by the roadside, her former youthfulness and energy withered away. She ate less and less; her body became emaciated. She could no longer walk. Finally, against the continued advice of his relatives and friends, Prem decided to take Laxmi to the mission hospital, not far from the mission school he had gone to years before.

Prem was a poor man, and he had no money to pay porters to carry Laxmi the day's journey to the hospital. So he carried her himself. By means of a single circle of rope flattened into a band across his forehead, he carried his wife piggyback up and down the two mountains that lay between his village and the hospital. He arrived at dusk and settled his wife on a straw mat in one of the nearby leaf-and-twig "hotels" that catered to patients waiting overnight to see the doctor.

At four the next morning Prem took Laxmi to the hospital waiting area to get in line for the registration office, which opened at eight o'clock. Already twenty patients with their family members had lined up; they had spent the night sleeping on the concrete floor outside the office. By the time the office opened, over a hundred patients were in line, accompanied by an equal number of family members, many of whom wanted to be examined themselves now that they were at the hospital. Like Prem and Laxmi, these people had walked or been carried an average of one day to reach the hospital.

Two doctors were on duty in the outpatient clinic that day, one of them being my wife Cynthia. When Laxmi's turn came up, it was Cynthia who examined her. Within a minute it was obvious to Cynthia that Laxmi was suffering from far-advanced tuberculosis. A chest x-ray confirmed the diagnosis. Cynthia admitted Laxmi to the hospital for one month of Streptomycin injections and other treatment. Prem had not reckoned on the length of hospitalization necessary, so early the next morning he returned to his home to fetch more food. He could not afford to buy food from the local shops for that long a period. Village Nepalis rarely have spare cash; they live off what their own land can produce.

Laxmi improved rapidly under treatment, and within the month she had become strong enough to walk home. On the day of discharge from the hospital, Cynthia carefully explained to Prem that Laxmi would have to continue taking the oral medicine without interruption for a total of eighteen months; if she didn't, the tuberculosis could recur in a form that would be resistant to treatment. Cynthia gave Laxmi an initial three-month supply of pills, and told Prem to return to get more just before the three months were up. Then Cynthia prayed for the couple and offered them a small tract about Jesus entitled, "Who Is He?" Prem, who had learned to read years earlier at the mission school, promised to read it to Laxmi. He had already read another similar tract at the hospital, and it had brought back to mind some of the things he had learned from his teachers years before. Cynthia then said to Prem, "There is no medical bill for you to pay. Laxmi's treatment has been free. And it will continue to be free as long as she continues taking the medicine without interruption. However, if she stops the medicine before the proper time and the tuberculosis recurs, any further treatment will not be free; you will have to pay for it. That is a hospital rule." Prem assured Cynthia that he would be back on time to get more medicine.

Laxmi continued getting better at home, and near the end of the three months, she felt completely well. Relatives and village friends scoffed at the idea of going back to the hospital to get more medicine. "Why should a well person need medicine?" they asked. Prem wavered, and finally decided that they were right. His wife was cured; that was plain to see.

Three more months passed, and then Prem noticed with alarm that Laxmi was beginning to cough again. Then the fever returned. Laxmi lost weight and became progressively weaker. Prem remembered Cynthia's warnings and realized his mistake. But now he was embarrassed to go back to the hospital. Besides, the treatment would no longer be free. The village shaman, initially silenced by Laxmi's apparent cure, now felt vindicated and told Prem that he should never have taken Laxmi to the hospital in the first place.

Two more months passed and Laxmi continued to get weaker. Prem knew that if he did nothing, she would die. So he determined to take her back to the hospital. He sold two goats to get the needed money. And on a drizzly monsoon day, he put Laxmi on his back and set out on the day's journey to the hospital.

Again Laxmi became Cynthia's patient. Cynthia restarted injections of Streptomycin. She added two new drugs to Laxmi's treatment regime. Laxmi again responded well to treatment. And Prem was filled with joy. Unlike most Nepali husbands we encountered at the hospital, he demonstrated great affection for his wife. Now, for the second time, she was being brought back from death to life. Prem promised he would not allow the treatment to be interrupted again. He learned to give injections so that he could continue Laxmi's Streptomycin at home. And during this time at the hospital Prem bought a Nepali New Testament and began to read it.

When it came time to leave the hospital, Prem was given the bill to pay. The ongoing treatment would cost still more money. The hospital had good reason for its policy of requiring payment for tuberculosis treatment the second time around. Some penalty was needed to motivate patients to be faithful in continuing their treatment, so that resistant strains of tuberculosis would not develop in the community at large. Those that were unfaithful in continuing their treatment were not only putting themselves at risk but many others as well. Prem understood this, and readily paid his bill. And when the three months of medicine Cynthia had ordered ran out, he came back to the hospital on time to get more.

However, the cost of the medicine was high for a village Nepali, and toward the end of the second three-month period Prem found himself in financial difficulty. Laxmi seemed healed. Cynthia had told him that Laxmi would need treatment for eighteen months, and Prem didn't see how he was going to pay for the remaining twelve months. Already he had sold all his goats; he couldn't sell his land. And so, in spite of his promise, Prem let Laxmi's treatment lapse a second time.

About this time a young American teacher came to live in Prem's village. Prem got to know him, and together they studied the New Testament that Prem had bought at the hospital. More than anyone else, this young teacher helped open Prem's eyes to the truth of the gospel. Prem grew in his understanding of the Christian faith. But all during this time, unbeknownst to him, Laxmi's tuberculosis was coming back. And suddenly, one day, she began coughing up blood.

Nepalis tend to be fatalistic. The natural reaction for a person in Prem's situation would have been to throw up one's hands and blame the gods. But something was different about Prem. Even from his youth, when he ran away to school, Prem had never been content to accept his circumstances passively. Driven by his deep love for Laxmi, and with the encouragement of the American school teacher, Prem decided against all odds to take his wife back to the hospital for the third time.

Again he arrived with his precious load after the one-day walk. Because Laxmi was having difficulty breathing and was continuing to cough up blood, Prem took her directly to the ward to be admitted as an emergency by the evening nursing staff. Cynthia was called from home to come and examine the new patient.

Cynthia walked the four minutes down the path from our house to the hospital. She immediately recognized Prem and Laxmi, and knew at once what had happened. Laxmi lay on the examining table fighting for breath. Prem stood by her head, tears in his eyes.

"Please save my wife," he said to Cynthia. "I can't bear to lose her."

Cynthia examined Laxmi. She knew she would not survive many days without treatment. But the larger question was: What treatment would she give? Once tuberculosis patients interrupt their course of treatment, the same drugs are usually not effective the second time around; resistance has developed, and new drugs are required. Indeed, a new drug, Rifampicin, had just become available, and we had a small supply at the hospital. However, it was exorbitantly expensive—indeed one hundred times more expensive than the drugs we usually used. Given the fact that we were a mission hospital with limited resources, we could have treated one hundred patients for the price of treating just one patient with Rifampicin. In addition, Laxmi had twice disregarded the doctor's careful instructions. Clearly the hospital could not subsidize such expensive medicine under these circumstances. Cynthia knew all this; and she also knew that Prem couldn't afford to pay for any kind of medicine—let alone Rifampicin, the only medicine that could save his wife.

Cynthia decided that the only solution would be for her to personally pay for Laxmi's medicine. She said to Prem, "You know that, according to the rules, the hospital cannot provide you with the expensive treatment Laxmi needs. However, because of your deep love for your wife, I have decided to pay for her treatment myself. We will admit her and begin treatment at once."

At this Prem broke down and wept with tears of joy.

Then Cynthia said to Laxmi, "You do not really deserve this last chance for life. Twice you have failed to follow the hospital rules. However, because of your husband's love for you, we are going to give you this one last chance."

Then Cynthia felt the Holy Spirit prompt her to add: "None of us deserves any mercy from God; none of us deserves to receive life. Because of our sinfulness the only thing any of us deserves is the sentence of death. But because of God's love for us, He has shown mercy toward us, and has forgiven our sins. Instead of giving us what we deserve—death—He has given us life through His Son Jesus Christ, who has paid the penalty for our sins. If you believe in Him, you will receive life that will never end."

Laxmi was too sick to comprehend Cynthia's meaning, but Prem nodded in agreement. For the first time he fully understood what God's love had done for him, what Christ had done for him, and he believed. All that he had heard, even from as far back as that mission school at age eleven, seemed to come together now, as he experienced this tangible demonstration of God's love for him and for his wife. A seed planted twenty years earlier, and watered by an American teacher, had now sprung up in true faith.

Laxmi recovered completely. Some time later, through the love and witness of her husband and other Christians, she too accepted Christ. Prem and Laxmi were the first of their Tibetan Buddhist tribe in our area of Nepal to become Christians. And today, through their testimony, others are following in their steps.

How Two British Women
Moved a People

Chapter Two

I t is one thing for two individual members of a tribe to accept Christ, as was the case with Prem and Laxmi. That is the way most people of Tibetan Buddhist background come to Christ—by ones and twos. But it is quite a different matter when large numbers of a tribe—even thousands—come to Christ in a short period of time. Such was the story of the Tamangs of western Nepal, one of the country's largest tribal groups. Their story begins in 1952, and it begins on the hot, dusty plains of northern India.

Lily O'Hanlon was a medical doctor from England who for over ten years had been working in a dispensary in the Indian town of Nautanwa, just south of the Nepal border. With her was an Irish agriculturist named Hilda Steele. Nautanwa was the railhead for Nepalis coming out of the hills to the north, and so there was a constant stream of Nepali travelers passing through the town on their way to and from India. Aside from those Nepalis who ventured outside their closed mountain kingdom, the outside world had virtually no contact with or knowledge of Nepal. Its border had been closed to foreigners for over one hundred years. Ten million people lived in Nepal, and not one of them was a Christian. The only chance they had to hear the gospel was when they came into the Indian border towns such as Nautanwa.

So Dr. Lily and Hilda, together with a few colleagues, formed the Nepal Evangelistic Band, and for many years this little band single-mindedly shared the gospel with as many Nepalis as they could meet. All during this time they longed for the day when they would be able to enter Nepal itself. On clear days they could look northward and see the nearby forest-covered hills, and then behind them higher and higher hills, and finally, barely visible in the distance, the white crest of the Himalayan Range etched across the skyline.

Then in 1952 the opportunity to enter Nepal finally came. A palace revolution had occurred in Kathmandu, the capital, and the ruling family of hereditary prime ministers had been ousted. This family, the Ranas, had ruled Nepal as their own private fiefdom for over a century, keeping the legitimate heirs to the Nepali throne under house arrest all that time. Now the current king had been reinstated, and one of his first official acts had been to invite the outside world to come into Nepal and aid in the development of the country. At that time Nepal was the poorest nation on earth, with the lowest standard of health in all the world. The average life expectancy was twenty-nine years. And so it was not surprising that when Lily O'Hanlon and Hilda Steele applied for permission to enter Nepal to do medical work, their request was soon granted. And in November, 1952, the two women, together with several other members of the Nepal Evangelistic Band, set out on foot across the India-Nepal border and headed northward up into the first tier of Himalayan foothills.

They walked for six days. Foot trails were the "highways" of Nepal in those days; roads were still unknown. The trail was rarely level; it ascended and descended ridge after ridge, mountain after mountain. Starting at nearly sea level, the party climbed to over 7,000 feet, and then climbed down again almost as far. And then up once more, and down. Each time the party reached a high point on the trail, they could see tiers of ridges in front of them, and in the distance, towering over all, the majestic snow-covered peaks of the Himalayas.

As the band walked along, Nepalis would come out of their thatch-roofed houses to stare at the foreigners. Many other Nepalis passed them on the trail: small children leading huge water buffalos; groups of women carrying their empty earthenware jugs to a nearby spring; farmers going to and from their fields balancing wooden ploughs across their shoulders; and mule trains laden with goods coming down from Tibet. When the party entered a village they would be held up for hours as the residents, having heard that a doctor was passing through, came in droves to be examined.

On seeing the condition of the people, Lily and Hilda felt as if they had been moved in time back into the Middle Ages. As they journeyed, they found nothing connected with the twentieth century; no electricity, no radios, no plumbing, no schools, no books—not even a wheel. The medical condition of the people was frightful. They saw

old folks blind with cataracts, young people with deformities from un-
treated burns, men and women with huge goiters, women with ovarian
cysts the size of watermelons, leprosy victims, people dying of tuberculosis, and on and on—conditions that in the West are seen only in old
medical-school textbooks. On every side the band encountered needs
crying out to be met, the greatest of them being the need of these Nepalis
to hear the good news of the gospel.

In spite of the immense physical need and abject poverty of the
people they encountered, Lily and Hilda were struck with the beauty
and quaintness of the scenery that confronted them at every turning of
the trail. They walked through forests of bamboo, past papaya and ba-
nana trees laden with fruit, up terraced rice paddies filled with golden
rice ready for harvesting. Troops of monkeys chattered at them as they
passed; and flocks of parakeets erupted from nearby trees, frightened
by the commotion of the passing party. The thatch-roofed villages dot-
ting the hillsides seemed content and clean from afar; mountain streams
babbled across the path; and always in the distance, yet nearer and
nearer, rose the mighty Himalayas, their summits shooting up above
the low-lying clouds.

On the sixth day the party reached the top of the last ridge, and
there beneath them lay the valley of Pokhara, one of the most fertile
and well-watered valleys in all of Nepal. And immediately across the
valley rose the Annapurna Massif, 26,000 feet high, one of the best-
known of the Himalayan Mountain groups. Indeed it was Annapurna
Mountain that was the first of the major Himalayan peaks to be climbed.
It was climbed by a Frenchman back in 1952, and he wrote a book
about it called *Annapurna*. I remember reading that book as a boy. And
so, back in 1952, the world sat up and took notice of what was happening up at the top of Annapurna Mountain—but it did not take any notice of what was happening down at its foot.

For Lily and Hilda and their team had gone down into that last valley
at the foot of Annapurna Mountain. They settled in the main town of the
valley, Pokhara. And one of the first things they did was to establish a hospital. They built their hospital using army-surplus Quonset huts made of shiny
aluminum; they placed the Quonset huts side by side in two rows on an open
square at one end of the town. Their hospital became known as the "Shining
Hospital," because as the Nepalis came down from the surrounding hills
they could see the sun reflecting off the tops of the aluminum huts.

The fame of the hospital grew quickly. Nepalis would come from a distance of two and three days' walk to see the mission doctor. Other Western doctors came to help. Eventually Lily returned to England, and Hilda moved to another part of Nepal. The hospital work continued to grow. A surgeon came, and high quality surgery was carried out. People began coming from as far away as India and Tibet to be treated at the Shining Hospital. And for over thirty years that hospital provided treatment to untold thousands of Nepali patients. Only in recent years has it finally been replaced by a new 150-bed government hospital.

One of those thousands of patients in the late 1960s was a Tamang tribesman who happened to be living in Pokhara, the town where the Shining Hospital was located. The Tamangs inhabit hundreds of villages throughout central Nepal. Their religion is Tibetan Buddhism, liberally sprinkled with elements of Hinduism and animism. This particular Tamang tribesman had become ill and had gone to the Shining Hospital, and the medical staff there had not only given him medicine, but they had also prayed for him, and he had recovered. In addition, the missionaries had given him a Nepali New Testament, and they had told him something about a living God who answers prayer and who can heal the sick.

A short time after this, a nephew of this tribesman came to visit from a Tamang village four days' walk away. This nephew, Lok Bahadur, had come on business of some sort—Pokhara was a major trading center—and so he stayed with his uncle. When Lok Bahadur's business was completed a few days later, he got ready to return the four-day walk to his own village. But before he left, his uncle told him about the experience he had had at the Shining Hospital, and about the living God who answered prayer and healed the sick. The uncle also showed Lok Bahadur the New Testament he had gotten at the hospital.

The uncle's understanding of the Christian faith was no doubt imprecise; furthermore, it was only with difficulty that he and his nephew were able to read this New Testament he'd been given. Nevertheless, when it came time for Lok Bahadur to return to his own village, he had become sufficiently interested in this new God of the missionaries that he took that New Testament back home along with him.

When Lok reached his own village after the four-day walk, he found that his daughter had become sick during his absence. His wife, on the advice of some relatives, had called in the leading shaman of the village, and for three nights in a row this shaman had carried out healing rituals, but to no avail. The girl had gotten steadily worse. The shaman planned more rituals.

Lok Bahadur then told his wife and friends what he had learned during his visit to Pokhara. He said that instead of paying more money to the shaman for treatment that wasn't working, they should try praying to the Christian God he had heard about. His relatives and neighbors scoffed at the idea, and chided him for disregarding the traditions of his tribe. However, Lok persisted, and when his neighbors became angry and abusive, he drove them out of his house.

That night, alone, Lok Bahadur prayed to an unknown and untried God, asking in Jesus' name that his daughter might be spared. He prayed for a long time and then finally fell asleep. In the morning his daughter was completely well.

The villagers were not impressed. They attributed the healing to the efforts of the shaman on the three preceding nights, and claimed that the healing had merely been delayed. Lok alone remained convinced that the Christian God had heard his prayer and had healed his daughter.

A few days later someone else in the village became sick. The shaman was again called in, but the sick person continued to get worse and worse. Lok Bahadur heard about it and offered to pray for the sick person just as he had prayed for his own daughter. Since the family was desperate, they agreed. So Lok came, and again prayed in Jesus' name, and by the next morning that sick person also had become completely well.

This second healing caused a great stir in the village. Some accused Lok of practicing witchcraft. The shaman said that Lok was in league with an evil spirit. Other villagers accused him of defiling their village by following a foreign religion. Some were just puzzled. But the family of the sick person believed in this new God, and refused to join the rest of the village in condemning Lok Bahadur.

Over the next several months a dozen similar healings occurred in response to the prayers of Lok Bahadur. One of those healed was the wife of Bir Bahadur, a village leader. She had been sick for several months with fever and cough, and despite the efforts of several shamans had been growing steadily weaker. Lok Bahadur offered to pray for Bir's wife, and when Bir agreed, Lok once more called on his God to heal the sick woman. The next morning the wife was much improved, and within three days she was completely healed. As a result, Bir Bahadur also began to believe in the Christian God.

Soon a dozen or more villagers had begun meeting together to worship this new and powerful God. Lok Bahadur read to them haltingly from the New Testament he had gotten from his uncle. True, they couldn't understand everything that was read, but they knew that this was a God who healed, and on this they based their faith. They stopped worshiping their old gods and gradually stopped taking part in the traditional religious observances of the community.

Inevitably the community turned against this fledgling group of Christians. The shamans and other village leaders began to harass and persecute them. Acts of vandalism were carried out against them, sporadically at first, but then more frequently. Their crops were stolen or destroyed, their fields were ravaged. They were threatened with beatings. One night a fire was set to one of their homes. And yet even under such persecution the number of believers continued to grow.

It is often remarked of Buddhists that they have a placid and tranquil temperament, that they remain above the common jealousies and conflicts that other people get caught up in, that they are kind and gentle and, above all, tolerant. But this small group of Christians saw another face of Buddhism that foreigners rarely see. The position of the shamans was being challenged by these upstart faith healers; the shamans' power to heal could not match the power of the Christian God, who seemed always to answer the prayers of these believers. And so, like the Pharisees of Jesus' day, they conspired to rid their town of these Christians one way or another.

It became increasingly difficult for the Christians to survive in their village. In the hills of Nepal if you don't grow your own food you don't eat; and so, with their crops being stolen or damaged season after season, the believers could barely put food on their plates. Lok Bahadur moved away, leaving Bir Bahadur the leader of the group, which had by this time grown to seventeen households.

Then one day the male members of the group were summoned to the village center by the shamans. When they had gathered, the shamans and their cohorts tied the Christians' hands behind their backs and began to beat them with wooden clubs. They then fined the believers a large sum of money and told them that if they continued to follow their new religion they would be beaten and fined again.

Shortly after this, Bir Bahadur and several others in the little group decided to leave their village for good. They had heard that the Nepali government had recently set aside a large tract of land in a neighboring district for the resettlement of landless people, and so they decided to start over on this new land. Four families agreed to go at first, with the other families to follow. They packed their few possessions and together set out westward to this land of opportunity and promise.

After three days of walking, they reached the long, waterless clay slopes of Duradara, uninhabited and uninviting. This was their destination, the "promised land" their government had set aside for them. Undaunted, they set about building temporary shelters of sticks and leaves, and then with their crude spades, they began to hack out terraces along the hard and rocky hillside. They chopped down scores of trees. When their fields were at last prepared, they planted their first crop of corn.

With the monsoon season fast approaching, the four families scurried to build rainproof houses for themselves. Mud and stones were plentiful for the walls, but there was no thatch available for the roofs, since that type of grass is cut only after the monsoon season is over. So they were forced to use leaves instead, a much inferior material, ensuring that their houses would be nearly as damp on the inside as they were on the outside.

They survived that first monsoon with their homes and spirits intact. They planted rice in the lower terraces where water was more abundant. They fished in the large river that flowed at the foot of their hillside. They cut down more trees, built more terraces. The remaining Christian families from their old village came and joined them. New houses went up, new fields were prepared, and the little band of settlers began to make a life for themselves on their new land. They had set out with virtually nothing—except their faith. Now this land had indeed become a land of promise. The Christian community of Duradara was born.

Their community prospered. They put into practice the basic New Testament teachings they had learned earlier. They helped each other; they were honest and hard working. They prayed together, and the sick continued to be healed. The settlers were at last free, and their stomachs full. Word of their circumstances began to reach the ears of the people back in their old village, and before long, other families came and joined them.

Soon members of the Duradara community began going back on missionary journeys to their original tribal area. Former neighbors, once their enemies, came to them to ask for prayer for their sick. Many were healed. News of these happenings began to spread to other Tamang villages, and people began believing in the Christian God, at first by ones and twos, then by tens and twenties, and finally by the hundreds. Many moved to Duradara to join the Christian community there. But most stayed in their own villages, winning their friends and neighbors to Christ through their love and joy, and through the healing power manifested when they went to their God in prayer.

During this period, one example of how the Christian influence spread was that of a young, slightly deranged woman named Flechya, who lived in a large village in the northern part of the Tamang region. She had married and had a son, but the son had died at the age of three, and Flechya's husband had accused her of being responsible for the child's death. He drove her out, claiming she was a witch. The villagers treated her no better; wherever she went she was jeered, beaten, even stoned. Indeed, the villagers were afraid of her. Her appearance was wild; she behaved like an animal.

But in her heart she was not an animal. She had heard of the Christian community at Duradara, and how people were healed there in response to prayer. She thought, "If only I could get to that place, they might help me." She had no other hope; Duradara was like a light, drawing her.

Eventually she reached Duradara. The Christians there did not mistreat her, they were not afraid of her. Instead, they loved her and cared for her. Through prayer, they brought her back to life and restored her to health mentally, emotionally and spiritually. Through these Christians, she met Jesus.

Flechya felt called to go back to her own village and tell others about the healing power of Christ. People came to see her, to see this amazing occurrence—a mad woman restored to her right mind. She was a present-day version of the demon-possessed man described in the Gospels, whose restoration led to the destruction of a herd of pigs.

The news of Flechya's healing spread rapidly. It couldn't be denied; so many people had known her in her demented state. She told others about Jesus. She prayed for people, and they were healed. She even healed animals. And today she is a leader of a growing Christian group in her village.

Through many individuals like Flechya, the influence of the Christians spread. Within a few years, dozens of Christian communities had sprung up throughout the Tamang region of western Nepal. Some of the shamans themselves came to faith in Christ, and burned their amulets and prayer wheels; and when they did so they brought hundreds of others with them. Entire villages were transformed. Other Tamangs could see the difference in these Christians: their communities were like lights set on the hills of Nepal.

Almost thirty years have passed since Lok Bahadur visited his uncle in Pokhara and heard about the Christian God for the first time, and today that first Christian community at Duradara has grown to over six hundred people. But more amazing than that, back in the original Tamang homeland there are now over forty thousand believers scattered in scores of villages throughout the region. The Tamang region in western Nepal is a particularly wild and inhospitable area, and the people were once wild and inhospitable too. The villages are perched on steep craggy ridges, with deep river gorges snaking thousands of feet below. Many years ago the king of Nepal sent a regiment of army soldiers to subdue the people, but the soldiers only advanced to the outskirts of the region. There, with the help of some local inhabitants they conscripted, they built a low stone wall demarcating the extent of the king's authority, the "end" of the kingdom of Nepal. The area to the north remained lawless and unsubdued.

But the kingdom of God knows no walls, no barriers. And today that wild and lawless region has come within God's kingdom. As you look across the steep hillsides at the little villages and their thatched houses, it is much easier to count the non-Christian homes than it is to count the Christian ones. The majority of the people have become Christians. The old Buddhist prayer flags still flutter in the wind, but the words written on them are no longer Buddhist prayers but verses from the Bible. The tridents on their houses have been replaced with crosses.

And how did this all come about? It came about because of that nephew, Lok Bahadur, who got the New Testament from his uncle, who had been treated by the missionaries at the mission hospital, which was there because Lily O'Hanlon and Hilda Steele had walked into Nepal in 1952. And indeed, that is only one story that can be traced back to Lily O'Hanlon and Hilda Steele. Our lives are like pebbles dropped into a pool, and the ripples go out and out and out.

So far, among Tibetan Buddhists, the Tamangs are the only group who have come to Christ in such large numbers. There are roughly twenty other tribal groups in Nepal who practice a form of Tibetan Buddhism, and many of them are still utterly unreached. Taken together, they total several million people. The Tamangs, too, have seen this need, but by themselves they have neither the training nor the resources to meet it. God is looking for a new Lily O'Hanlon and a new Hilda Steele. As in the case of the Tamangs, God is able to do mighty works, but He chooses to use us to get the ball rolling.

MISSIONARIES—WESTERN AND EASTERN

CHAPTER THREE

In an earlier day, missionaries tended to be stereotyped: the evangelist, sober and serious, with Bible in hand; the doctor or nurse caring for the sick in a sweltering tropical hospital; the scholarly translator, pale and thin, peering at dimly lit piles of paper on a cluttered table. Common to all the above was a sense of earnestness, of urgency, even of humorlessness. Missionaries had a certain otherworldliness about them, a decorum, which set them apart from normal Christians: plain clothes, plain speech, plain manners. The mission field was no place for frills—much less, flamboyance.

Enter Eva Schmidt, one of the greatest missionary stereotype smashers of all time.

I first met Eva in 1987. I was sitting quietly minding my own business in a restaurant in a certain Asian city—which shall go unnamed—and was about to get up to leave for a meeting I was to attend, when in walked Eva. I knew it must be she from things I'd been told about her—things divulged in shocked yet approving tones, like enticing appetizers before the main course arrives.

I was not disappointed; in fact, the verbal descriptions fell short of the reality. Eva swept into the restaurant looking like she'd just done a video for MTV, sat down at my table, and proceeded to talk nonstop for the next half hour, making me late for my meeting in the process. It was worth it.

Eva was an attractive woman in her late thirties, with long, flowing blond hair and the attire of a gypsy dancer. If her high-school class had given a prize for "Most Vivacious," Eva would have won it. At the time I met her, Eva was shepherding a Tibetan congregation, running an orphanage, lecturing in church training programs, and generally befriending and encouraging any Christian worker who got within ear-shot. Already she had been a missionary among Tibetans in this city for seventeen years.

Eva was from Germany, where her parents taught in a Christian school. She had come to faith as a child. At age ten she read a book called *High Adventure in Tibet*, written by a man who had trekked three years across Tibet and suffered unimaginable hardships during his journey. As a result of reading that book, Eva decided that God wanted her to go to Tibet as a missionary.

For many missionaries, a desire for adventure is part of their call. By itself, the desire for adventure is not a valid reason for becoming a missionary; but when it is combined with other signs of God's leading, it can prove to be a very valuable gift—certainly if one is thinking to work among Tibetan Buddhists. Eva had that gift.

With adventure comes danger. It has been observed that a higher than usual proportion of those working among Tibetan Buddhists come to some kind of physical harm. Shortly before I met Eva that first time, a young couple with five children had been killed in a plane crash as their plane attempted to land in the city where Eva worked. The couple's ministry had been evangelism among Tibetans, and they were particularly gifted for it and committed to it. It was Eva herself who had urged them to take a brief holiday from the pressure of their work; it was on returning from that holiday that their plane crashed.

A Danish missionary crossing from Tibet into Nepal got caught in a freak landslide and perished. Others have been stricken with strange illnesses, which disappeared when they ceased their ministry. One Norwegian working with Tibetan Buddhists in Kathmandu was fixing a neighbor's roof when a gust of wind blew him off; the resulting fall left him paralyzed from the waist down. That very same gust of wind with its accompanying hailstones had also caused a panic in Kathmandu's main sports stadium, resulting in over a hundred deaths as people stampeded for the exits. It was an ill wind by any measure. The Norwegian was flown to Norway for treatment, but his paralysis remained unchanged. Nonetheless, six months later he returned to resume his work in Kathmandu, getting around by means of a wheelchair and a specially outfitted three-wheel, diesel-run vehicle. Within another six months, he was dead of metastatic skin cancer—a totally unrelated condition.

No one would call any of this "adventure." But it is very much a part of missionary work, and Tibetan Buddhist work in particular. This is why supporters on the home front must pray for their missionaries, and why missionaries should not go out until such prayer support is assured.

Eva may have originally been drawn by the adventure that Tibet promised, but she quickly came to know of the dangers as well. Many of them she would experience first hand.

Eva made her first trek into Tibet in 1985, a time when it was still illegal to travel in most parts of the country. Trekking in the high mountain passes of Tibet is exhausting; the altitude is often over 12,000 feet and the trails rise and fall precipitously. One spots a tiny hamlet a thousand feet up on the side of a narrow gorge. You don't feel like climbing up there, but you have to, for that is why you came.

In every village a new experience, a new opportunity awaited. Often it was an opportunity to perform some practical service that would give an entree into the hearts of the people. In other cases it would be the opportunity to share a word or a tract.

On that first trip into Tibet, Eva met an elderly man in one village who told her he was not satisfied with his Tibetan Buddhist religion. Eva gave him a tract.

Later that day Eva found the man and asked him, "Did you understand what you read in the pamphlet I gave you?"

The man answered, "Yes, I did. Over thirty years ago I stopped worshiping idols. I was sure that somewhere there was a God who was not an idol. Then the Chinese invaded our country and destroyed all our idols. Our idols couldn't have meant anything; suddenly they were gone. I was even more sure after that that there must be some creator god who is real and powerful. And then I read your booklet, and I thought, 'This must be true; this must be the God I have been searching for.'"

Eva said, "Will you believe in Him?"

"No."

"Why not?" asked Eva.

The man answered, "I am too old. Why didn't you come thirty years ago? I have been praying for thirty years to know this God, but now I am too old to change. I cannot learn a new religion now."

Eva said, "I couldn't come thirty years ago. I was only born thirty years ago. But my birth is an answer to your prayer. And here I am."

"It is still too late for me. I can't learn a whole new set of rules."

"There are no rules," said Eva. "All you have to do is believe." And that day Eva led the old man to faith in Christ.

There are many others like this old man, living in places you'd least expect. This is the harvest that Jesus said was ripe for picking; all that's needed are the pickers.

Eva's adventures during repeated subsequent trips into Tibet sound like a list of Paul's trials from 2 Corinthians. I hope one day somebody writes them down; they would fill a book. Eva has suffered from hunger and cold, arrest and imprisonment. She has been threatened, chased, robbed. She has trekked miles over high mountain passes and crossed dangerous rivers. She has suffered loneliness and illness. And through it all, God has sustained her and enabled her to bear much fruit to His glory. Hers is a story of courage, perseverance, and faith. Through Eva's life, and through the lives of others like her, the Book of Acts is still being written today.

I ran into Eva a second time in April, 1990. A revolution had just occurred in Eva's country, which brought partial religious freedom in its wake. A week later, at Easter, the Christians in the land celebrated by marching through the streets in a victory parade. Every church in Eva's city was represented, each congregation marching together holding aloft banners proclaiming Christ's victory. Eva's Tibetan congregation was marching too. I happened to be there that day. I spotted a group of fifty Tibetans clothed in their traditional costumes, and at their head was Eva, wearing a preposterous black wig and dressed, as ever, like a gypsy.

I went up to her and asked, "Why the black wig?"

"Oh, I wear it occasionally to make it less obvious that I'm a foreigner. My blond hair stands out, you know."

As if this monstrous wig didn't stand out; it could have been spotted from the space station. And even at that it was barely doing its job.

"I still see quite a bit of blond hair," I said, pointing to billows of golden locks cascading down from beneath the wig.

"Oh, yes," Eva said carelessly, "the thing keeps sliding up my forehead." And the parade passed on.

This book, however, is not only about Western missionaries who have gone into the Tibetan Buddhist world, but about Eastern missionaries as well—Tibetan Buddhists who have come to Christ and then gone on to serve as missionaries among their own people. What follows is the story of one of these missionaries.

At the mission hospital at Amp Pipal, where my wife Cynthia and I worked from 1970 to 1982, we relied on a succession of trained Nepali nurses to provide the backbone of our nursing service. They usually came for a one-to-two-year assignment. These young women were trained either in the mission nursing school in Kathmandu or in one of the Nepali government training programs. The first of these nurses to be assigned to the Amp Pipal Hospital back in 1973 was a bright and competent young Tibetan woman, whose grandparents had migrated from Tibet to Nepal many years before. She was pretty and petite, with long black hair and a clear complexion. She was also brisk, efficient and assured, giving both doctors and patients alike the sense that everything was under control.

Looking back over many years and many nurses, I can say that we never had a better nurse than Pasang Lama. This is high praise, because the great majority of Nepali nurses I have known have been well-trained and could have held their own anywhere in the world. Pasang did not seem phased by our primitive conditions, by live chickens tied under the patients' beds, by patients lying on benches (when we ran out of beds) and on straw mats (when we ran out of benches). She made the best of the situation she found, and in the process she set a high standard of nursing care, which thousands of our patients have enjoyed ever since.

Pasang was born in 1951 in a small, Tibetan-speaking village perched on the edge of the Arun River gorge just on the Nepal side of the Nepal-Tibet border. Her father was a trader, plying the high mountain trade routes between Tibet and India. Pasang never even heard of Christ until she was twelve; and she might not have heard of Him then were it not for the fact that her father, through his frequent travels, had become familiar with life and customs in Nepal and India.

When Pasang was seven her mother died, and she and a cousin were sent to a Nepali-language secondary school in India, an eight-day journey over difficult mountain trails. She and her cousin were the first two girls ever to leave their village to go to school. The school had been established by Roman Catholic missionaries in the Nepali-speaking region of northeastern India, and the languages used in the school were Nepali, Hindi, and English—but not Tibetan. Since it was a Nepali-medium school, Pasang soon became fluent in Nepali. She also became fluent in English.

Pasang had been at that school for two years, when one night she had a vivid and frightening dream. In the dream she saw the place where her childhood home had been, and her house was nothing but a pile of stones. Pasang attached no significance to the dream at the time, but several weeks later the 1962 border war between China and India broke out, and she was forced to flee back to her home village. When she arrived after nearly a week of arduous walking, she found that the Arun River had eroded its banks some weeks before, and many of the houses at its edge, including her family's home, had collapsed. What she found corresponded exactly to what she had seen in her dream.

After the China-India war was over, Pasang returned to her school and resumed her education. Her father had remarried the preceding year, but with the loss of his home, he had fallen into financial straits. The family of his new wife had bought property in far-off Kathmandu, the growing capital of Nepal, and so his wife's parents urged the father to move to Kathmandu and start a new life there.

Pasang spent seven years at that school. When she reached her final year, she was at the top of her class. A reasonable performance on the final exams would assure her of first place and an open door to further education anywhere she chose. She felt under intense pressure. During the economics exam she saw her classmates all around her cheating, looking up information in books and sharing answers with each other. Pasang became hesitant and confused. For one-half hour she could not concentrate, she couldn't even write. And when the final grades came in, Pasang's poor performance on the economics exam had pulled her down out of first place, and she ended up in the second division, a merely "above-average" student. For a female student, this was enough to close the door to further educational opportunities.

During the last few days at school, as Pasang was packing up her few belongings, she confided in one of her teachers, Mother Teresa, that she desired to become a Christian. So the Mother took Pasang into the school chapel and prayed with her that her desire might be fulfilled. Pasang's father had already arrived to take her to Kathmandu with him, but he declined Mother Teresa's invitation to enter the chapel; he waited outside the gate.

Compared to her school, which was at over 6,500 feet elevation, Kathmandu at 4,500 feet was a hot and sticky place. Flies, mosquitos, pollution and crowding—these things oppressed Pasang and her family. Above all, she couldn't find a job. She was not qualified for anything. At that time, 1968, thousands of jobless young people were roaming the streets of Kathmandu searching for work; what chance would she have among so many—and being a Tibetan at that?

One of the missions in Kathmandu had recently opened a girl's high school, and Pasang decided to go there and apply for a teaching job. The headmistress, a kindly woman from England, said to her, "My dear, you are just out of high school. You don't have the qualifications to be a teacher. Instead, why don't you go to the mission hospital and try to get a job as an interpreter. They have many English-speaking doctors there who don't understand Nepali; your English is good, so you could interpret for them when they speak with their Nepali patients."

So Pasang went to the mission hospital in Kathmandu, at that time the leading hospital in all of Nepal. They didn't need interpreters, she was told. But the American hospital administrator said to her, "Would you like to become a nurse?" The mission had just opened Nepal's first nursing school adjacent to the hospital compound. There were few Nepali girls at that time who were qualified to enter a nursing school. Even though the term had already begun three weeks earlier, the administrator felt that Pasang was capable of completing the course.

Pasang was desperate by this time. She had never thought about nursing, and had no idea how she could finance it, but she said, "Yes, I would like to become a nurse." And so the administrator called the nursing school director, also an American missionary, and she arranged for Pasang to begin classes the next day.

So much study needed! Nursing was not just bedpans and bandages. Pasang applied herself diligently and quickly caught up to the rest of the class. She soon made friends. A few of her classmates were Christians, and they welcomed her warmly. The missionary teachers also showed much love to her. She felt like part of a family. Weekly Christian fellowship meetings were held near the nursing school, and Pasang enjoyed the singing and the Bible studies. One of the most comforting things she learned was that there was hope in life after death; one didn't have to go to hell. Those who led the Bible studies spoke plainly and with authority. Pasang wrote back to Mother Teresa at her former school and said that she had become a Christian.

Toward the end of Pasang's first year in nursing school, her father and stepmother moved from Kathmandu to a city in eastern Nepal. So when the next school holiday came up, Pasang had nowhere to go. An American girl named Katherine, who was working in Kathmandu with Operation Mobilization (OM), visited Pasang at the nursing campus hostel and invited her to the OM home to spend her holiday. Pasang was more than happy to accept the invitation.

During that month's holiday Katherine taught Pasang things from the Bible that were deeper than anything she had heard before. Her sins seemed so black; how could Christ save her? What did she need to do? She was filled with fear that whatever she did, it would not be enough to save her from hell.

One night, as Pasang was wrestling with her fear alone in her room, an Indian girl on the OM staff named Karuna came and knocked on her door. When Pasang had asked her in, Karuna said to her, "Have you accepted Christ?"

Pasang answered, "I do not know if I have."

Then Karuna told Pasang how she herself had been fearful of death and hell throughout her childhood. She had tried to do what was right according to Hindu beliefs, but she never had the assurance it would be enough to save her. Then she heard about Christ, and immediately knew it was the truth. So she had simply accepted Christ and what He had done to cleanse her from her sins and free her from the fear of death. She didn't have to "do" anything, only to believe, to accept what Christ had done for her. Karuna told Pasang, "When I had done that, when I had simply accepted Christ, I was flooded with peace and joy. And that can be your experience too."

After Karuna left, Pasang thought to herself, "I don't need to follow rules; I don't need to endure hardships. All I need to do is to accept Christ."

Pasang began to visualize how Jesus had suffered and died for her. She felt Jesus drawing near to her. Outside, a furious monsoon storm raged with thunder and lightning. Pasang confessed her sins to Jesus, and asked Him to come into her life. And she immediately found freedom and joy and peace. She looked at her watch: the time was 8:45 p.m., August 24, 1971.

Pasang finished her nursing course, worked one year at the mission hospital in Kathmandu, and then came out to our hospital at Amp Pipal as our first fully qualified, Nepal-trained nurse.

After working with us for two years, Pasang returned to Kathmandu to teach in the mission nursing school. She lived in the hostel with the students, and became totally absorbed in the activities of the nursing campus. After several years she received a mission scholarship to get a graduate degree in nursing. But she had no sooner started the course when the vision in her left eye began to deteriorate rapidly. She saw eye doctors in Kathmandu, but they could do nothing for her. She was told that she had macular degeneration and needed a retinal specialist; the nearest one was in Delhi, India, five hundred miles away. She was advised to go there.

In 1980, through the provision of a Nepali Christian lady, Pasang was able to go to Delhi to get the needed treatment for her eye condition. However, a number of treatments were required, which necessitated a prolonged stay in Delhi. So Pasang got a job at a local hospital, putting to use the Hindi she had learned in high school. She ended up staying four years. During this period both her spiritual and her physical health declined and, as she herself said, she "drew far from the Lord."

During Pasang's final months in Delhi, she tried to join a group of young Indian professionals who were headed for the Middle East to work at salaries many times what they could get in India. But because Pasang was not an Indian citizen, she was disqualified. With this door closed to her, she decided to return to Nepal, broken in spirit and in health.

Things did not improve in Nepal. She was embarrassed to associate with her former Christian friends, and sought to avoid them. She wanted to maintain her independence, to do what she wanted rather than what others wanted. She got a job at a government hospital in Kathmandu, where working conditions were very poor. She never went to church. She was lonely and unhappy. Yet all through this period she was able to deceive herself into thinking that there was nothing really wrong.

Then during one of her lowest spiritual points, Pasang met two young Christian women, Margaret from Norway and Claire from New Zealand, who were working among Tibetans in Nepal. They invited her to their apartment for tea. And they kept on inviting her and befriending her; and God used them to bring Pasang back into fellowship with Christ and with other believers. In Pasang's words, "Margaret and Claire were angels sent to me by God." Margaret and Claire remind me of Jim Elliot's prayer: "Lord, make me a fork in people's paths rather than just a milestone along their journey." Margaret and Claire were such a "fork" in Pasang's path, and God used them to steer Pasang in a new direction.

Part of the redirecting process involved an illness. One day a nursing colleague told Pasang that her eyes were yellow. She had not been feeling well for several days and this explained it: infectious hepatitis. She was admitted at once to an infectious disease hospital on the outskirts of Kathmandu, where she promptly proceeded to get worse. She was put in the general ward along with twenty other patients. The hospital was understaffed, the toilets were filthy, and the ward was noisy, with nurses and patients shouting at each other both day and night. Pasang couldn't sleep. She was burning up with a raging fever, not a typical finding in hepatitis. She thought she was going to die. She cried out to God, "Give me another chance." For so long she had followed her own desires instead of God's, and she feared that she was going to lose her soul, her salvation. She remembered Jesus' words: "What good is it for a man to gain the whole world, yet forfeit his soul?" (Mark 8:36). And in her heart she repented of her willfulness, of her rebellion against God.

The next day Pasang's doctors decided that she not only had hepatitis but was also suffering from a far-advanced case of typhoid fever. They started treatment for the typhoid fever immediately, and within a couple of days the crisis was over and Pasang was out of danger.

Meanwhile Margaret had learned that Pasang had been taken to the infectious disease hospital, so she came and visited her. Margaret asked Pasang, "What is God saying to you now?"

Pasang answered, "God is telling me to begin serving Him again, and I am ready to do so."

Pasang quickly recovered after that. She regained her physical life and also her spiritual life. She felt ready for anything.

"Anything" turned out to be Bible college in Auckland, New Zealand, for the next two and a half years. Pasang's friend Claire had studied there, and she helped Pasang make the necessary arrangements for enrolling in the college. While there, Pasang received a clear call to undertake an evangelistic ministry among Tibetan people.

After returning from New Zealand in 1989, she joined an organization which was starting a work among Tibetan refugees in Nepal. She is the first national worker to join this organization; the other members are from a variety of outside countries. Having all her life been a recipient of the caring and the ministry of missionaries, Pasang is now a missionary in her own right, a witness to her own Tibetan people. She is helping to start a vocational training school for young Tibetans; she has begun translating Christian books into Tibetan; and she is personally sharing her faith in the Tibetan refugee camps and elsewhere in Nepal.

It has been rightly said that a missionary's task is not merely to lead people to Christ but to make people missionaries for Christ. As Pasang passes on to others the blessing she has received, may she in turn make new missionaries from among her own people, who will join her in bringing the gospel of Christ to all Tibetans.

An Orphan's Pilgrimage

Chapter Four

Another Tibetan missionary I have known is Pema Wangmo. Pema was born into a wealthy and prominent family in Lhasa, Tibet, in 1954. Three years later her father was killed in the war between China and Tibet, which ultimately resulted in the annexation of Tibet by China in 1959. Shortly after her father's death, Pema was taken from her mother by an aunt and subsequently raised by her, together with the aunt's own son, who was a few months younger than Pema.

In 1959, with the Chinese occupation of Tibet imminent, this aunt and her husband decided to go south into Nepal and India, and they took Pema and their son along with them. They rode on horses over the high Himalayan mountain passes. They journeyed to the city of Kalimpong in northern India, a popular destination for Tibetans fleeing the Chinese Communists.

After only a few months in Kalimpong, Pema's aunt took her son and returned to Tibet. Pema herself didn't know the reason for her aunt's going, but in any event, the Chinese army completed its occupation of Tibet shortly thereafter, and the aunt was unable to leave the country. And so Pema was left in the care of her aunt's husband, her uncle.

This uncle was a cruel man, and he forced Pema to become his personal servant. He beat her whenever he was displeased, and he let her go days without providing her with a proper meal. He would leave Pema alone for several days at a time, instructing her before he left that she was not to leave the house. So Pema, only seven years old, would spend days alone in the unheated house in Kalimpong with inadequate clothing, afraid to go out, afraid to call to the neighbors for help. Even the neighbors feared the anger of this heartless man.

When Pema was eight, her uncle left her for good, and she went to live at a nearby inn run by one of the neighbors. She was put to work baby-sitting and cleaning; her work day would begin at 4:00 a.m. and continue until late at night. She was given enough food, but no new clothes. Her clothes became progressively more worn and tattered, and during the winter months they were not sufficient to protect her from the cold at Kalimpong's 6,000-foot altitude. Since Pema could earn a few pice as tips from time to time, she saved up the money to buy bits of cloth, and she laboriously stitched them together to provide a supplement to the rags she was wearing.

After Pema had worked at the inn for almost two years, her aunt unexpectedly showed up in Kalimpong together with her son. She had escaped from Tibet, eluding the Chinese border guards stationed at the main Himalayan passes by taking little-known and dangerous trails over the mountains. After searching for Pema for some time, the aunt arrived at the inn where Pema was working, and called out, "Pema."

Pema went and stood before her aunt, but said nothing. Though her aunt's face was slightly familiar, Pema could not at first place her. Then Pema saw her aunt's son, and flushed. The boy cried out, "Acha," which means older sister. Then all at once Pema recognized her aunt and the boy with whom she had grown up.

The aunt then said, "I have come to take you. I will be back at three o'clock this afternoon and pick you up."

The inn owner's elderly mother had largely taken charge of Pema during her stay at the inn, and having heard what the aunt had said, the old woman then came to Pema and said, "Do not go with that person; you will be severely beaten if you try to leave here."

Exactly at three the aunt showed up, and without a word to anyone she grabbed Pema by the hand and led her out to a waiting taxi. They drove to a hotel across town where the aunt gave Pema a hot bath and some new clothes she had brought from Lhasa. When the girl was clean and dressed, her aunt sat her down in their hotel room and listened to Pema's story of her life at the inn and the suffering and deprivation she had endured. The aunt said nothing, only wept.

A few days later, the aunt took her son and Pema to Kathmandu, Nepal, where they settled near a major Buddhist shrine. There they stayed for more than two years; Pema's aunt worked as a seamstress to earn money to meet their needs. Then one day the aunt heard that the

Dalai Lama had opened an orphanage in Dharmsala in northern India, and she decided to put both her son and Pema in the orphanage.

The journey to Dharmsala took a week. As soon as her aunt had left to return to Kathmandu, the caretaker of the orphanage took Pema's new clothes that her aunt had given her and replaced them with a nondescript uniform which all the children were required to wear. Pema, after two years of relative happiness living with her aunt, now found herself again in a strange and unfriendly place. This orphanage seemed to function mainly as a clearing house for displaced Tibetan children. Once the youngsters had arrived and been processed, they were then sent out all over the world to be adopted.

After several months at Dharmsala, Pema was adopted by an elderly British missionary woman named Helen Paige, and taken to a children's home she ran in Gorakhpur, a medium-sized city on the Ganges Plain in northern India. This home was known as the Gorakhpur Nurseries, one of the best-known Christian orphanages on the Indian subcontinent. Here Pema was placed in a dormitory with six other Tibetan girls.

Pema was twelve years old when she arrived at Gorakhpur. The seven Tibetan girls felt set apart from the other three hundred children at the Nurseries. They were placed in a room by themselves. They were given Tibetan frocks to wear, whereas all the other girls were dressed in the usual Indian sari. These frocks would have been useful during the cold winter days Pema had spent at the higher elevations in Kalimpong and Kathmandu, but here at sea level on the stifling Ganges Plain the frocks were insufferably hot. Pema thought she would die of the heat, and spent every possible moment out under the shade of the trees that lined the compound.

Worse than the heat was the snickering and snide comments directed at the Tibetans by the other girls. The missionary staff seemed not to notice. Though the Tibetan girls struggled to learn Hindi, their distinctive accent and manner of speaking were mocked by the others. The teasing was mean and relentless, and got worse over the years as the girls passed up through junior high school. The ill-feeling of the other girls was aggravated by the Tibetans' refusal to take part in Christian festivals and worship. Several times Pema, along with two of her Tibetan girlfriends, threatened to run away, but having no place to go, they stayed on at the Nurseries and suffered in silence.

During her latter years at Gorakhpur, Pema became increasingly interested in the Christian faith of the missionaries who ran the Nurseries, but this interest did not develop into true faith while she was there. Outwardly she behaved like a Christian, but inwardly she remained hardened and angry toward her tormentors.

In 1967, when Pema was thirteen, she and two other Tibetan girls were sent to high school in Kanpur, a large Indian city nearby. There they were put in a hostel with other Tibetan students, also refugees from Chinese-occupied Tibet. These other students were offended that Pema had left her Buddhist traditions and seemed to be following the Christian religion. They began to malign her and mistreat her far more vehemently than the Hindu girls had done back at the Nurseries. Day after day her fellow students reduced Pema to tears, even going so far as to throw stones at her when no one was looking. The matrons at the hostel would ask Pema why she was crying, but whenever she gave the real reason, the other Tibetans denied it and accused her of lying. So she gradually ceased telling the matrons, and withdrew more and more into herself. And as she withdrew from the others, she found herself drawing closer and closer to Christ.

After two years at Kanpur, Pema was transferred to a Canadian mission school in Jhansi, another large Indian city about 150 miles from Kanpur, where she was to finish her last two years of high school. Here the persecution from her fellow students was much less, and she was greatly encouraged in her faith by one of her Christian teachers. But underneath, she was still rebelling against God, rebelling against the school discipline and especially against the strict chief matron, whom the girls had nicknamed "Naagin," the Hindi word for a female cobra. Pema had many run-ins with this matron, and finally threatened to leave the school. At that, the school principal and several senior teachers came to Pema and comforted her and encouraged her to stay.

Pema did stay and soon was into her final high-school year. Though outwardly she continued as a Christian, inwardly she experienced a terrible emptiness. Her faith gave her no real solace, no meaning to her life. She heard the other girls talk about their parents, their families, but Pema had no one to talk about, no one to remember except her aunt. Long ago in Kathmandu her aunt had given Pema a small mounted photograph of her real mother, which Pema had managed to keep safely all through the years in India. From time to time Pema would get her mother's picture out and gaze at it, and wonder where she was and whether she was even alive.

In the spring of 1971, Pema graduated from the Canadian mission school at Jhansi. She had made no definite plans about what she would do after graduation, but all through her senior year she had had a vague but growing desire to find her mother and be reunited with her. She decided to start her search in Kathmandu, for that was the city she best recollected from her childhood. Perhaps her aunt was still there as well. So in May, 1971, Pema came to Kathmandu.

Shortly after arriving, Pema heard about a nursing school that had recently been opened by one of the missions operating in Nepal. It was the same nursing school that Pasang Lama had entered the previous year. Pema went to inquire about enrolling in the school, and was immediately given a place, as the school year was just then beginning. The mission agreed to help her with a partial scholarship and a campus job. So with no advance preparation or even forethought, Pema suddenly found herself embarking on a new career, and not an easy one at that. With no knowledge of Nepali and little of English, she was barely able to keep up with her class. And her only reason for coming to Kathmandu in the first place had been to find her mother!

On one of Pema's first free weekends, she went to a Tibetan refugee camp located in Kathmandu not far from the nursing campus in order to make inquiries about her family. As she walked through the camp she held out the little photograph of her mother which her aunt had given her years before. Pema had lost most of her facility in the Tibetan language, which she had spoken as a child; she remembered a few words, but mainly she simply showed her mother's photograph to Tibetans she met. Most just shook their heads.

After a time Pema saw an old Tibetan man sitting by the main road just outside the camp. When she showed him the photograph, he said, "I know that lady." And pointing down a small side street he said, "Go there, and you will find her."

Pema went down the street the old man had indicated and showed the photo to the next person she met. That person also said, "Yes, I know this woman. Keep going down this street."

Next Pema saw two young girls about eight and ten years old playing in the street. Pema showed the girls the photo.

"That's our mother," the older one exclaimed. "How did you get that picture?"

In halting Tibetan, Pema briefly told her story.

"You are our older sister!" the girl said. "We have heard about you." And Pema hugged her two sisters there on the street.

Then the three of them together went to the girls' house, and found their mother washing her hair. The mother wrapped a towel around her head and came out to see what the girls wanted. When Pema saw her mother's face, she saw the likeness of her own face, and at once she knew beyond doubt that it was her mother.

"This is our sister," said the younger girl. And the mother immediately recognized Pema, and embraced her.

For some minutes they hugged each other, and cried, and hugged some more. Pema could barely understand what her mother and sisters were saying, and even less could she express her own feelings. But finally she had found her family; she was an orphan no longer.

Just then the young girls' father came up, Pema's stepfather, whom her mother had married in 1962, several years after Pema had left Tibet with her aunt. At first Pema thought it was her real father; she had never been told that her own father had been killed in the China-Tibet war. Nonetheless, the stepfather welcomed Pema warmly. Immediately he announced that the family would go to Baudha, the great stupa in Kathmandu, and give thanks to the gods for Pema's return.

Perhaps Pema did not fully understand her stepfather's intentions. At any rate, when the family arrived at the stupa, Pema declined to walk clockwise around the huge structure in the usual fashion, but instead went in the opposite direction. She also refused to bow down. Her mother and stepfather were embarrassed and perplexed. "Why are you dishonoring the gods by not worshiping in the proper way?" her mother asked.

Pema answered, "Because I have become a Christian."

The following weekend Pema again went to the Tibetan camp to visit her family. Again her stepfather insisted they go to the stupa to worship. And once again Pema refused to bow down and worship gods in whom she no longer believed. After that, her mother and stepfather became very cool toward her. They acted as if she had insulted them, even betrayed them. Pema went to see them a few more times, but she did not feel welcome. Her visits became infrequent.

Meanwhile, Pema was feeling the pressure of nursing school. She had barely enough money to survive. Her family urged her to quit nursing school and get a good-paying job and help support them financially. But Pema determined to continue her nursing training and stubbornly refused to ask for help from anyone.

During nursing school Pema's spiritual growth as a Christian progressed only slowly. She thought she was a good Christian, but because of difficulty in the language (her main language was Hindi) and unfamiliarity with Nepali culture, she did not make friends readily and failed to find close fellowship with other Christians. Furthermore, she had asked to be baptized, but had been refused. She was told Tibetans needed to be eighteen years old to be baptized, and Pema was only seventeen. Discouraged, she did not pursue the matter again during her nursing school training.

A final blow came at the end of nursing school, when she was denied a nursing certificate by the Nepali government because she was not a Nepali citizen. Four years of hard study and sacrifice had counted for nothing. The mission, however, appealed to the government to reverse this unjust decision, and eventually the queen of Nepal herself granted Pema her nursing certificate.

After receiving her certificate, Pema worked for one year at a mission hospital a day's journey southwest of Kathmandu, and there she began to make friends with Christian fellow workers. She became eager for serious Bible study, though on her own she had difficulty understanding what she read. Toward the end of that first year after nursing school, April 10, 1976, Pema was baptized and officially accepted into the Christian fellowship. Finally she had found her true family.

Later that year Pema returned to Kathmandu and began working in the large mission hospital on the southern outskirts of the city, not far from the Tibetan camp where her mother and stepfather lived. Her mother, meanwhile, had become ill with advanced cancer; so Pema moved to the camp to care for her, while at the same time carrying out her hospital duties. The stepfather blamed the mother's illness on Pema; he claimed she had angered the gods by refusing to worship them properly. Even during her mother's final days, Pema refused to worship at the stupa, thus bringing on herself the enmity of the entire Tibetan population of the camp. People spat at her, abused her, and called her a prostitute and a witch. Children threw stones at her, with the encouragement of their elders. Pema hated to even walk through the camp, and whenever she did so she held her head down to avoid meeting the gaze of others. Finally her mother died, and the elder of her two younger sisters carried out the funeral rites. Thereafter her sisters and her stepfather spoke barely a word to her, even though she continued to live in her stepfather's house where she had moved during her mother's illness. For seven years she lived in this manner.

During those seven years Pema's faith was tested. Many times she thought, "I should give up this Christian religion. It has brought me nothing but persecution from my own people." But God held Pema in a special way. Every time people mistreated her, she remembered Jesus' words from the cross: "Father, forgive them, for they do not know what they are doing" (Luke 23:34). That became Pema's repeated prayer. Pema learned in a way few of us ever do what Jesus meant when He said, ". . . take up [your] cross daily and follow me" (Luke 9:23).

During those seven dark years God was preparing Pema for the next stage of her spiritual pilgrimage. Among Pema's small circle of Christian acquaintances in Kathmandu was a missionary from Korea, who offered to arrange for Pema to go to Seoul for theological training. So in 1984 Pema set off for Korea with a three-year scholarship to study at ACTS, the Asian Center for Theological Studies in Seoul.

In Pema's own words, arriving in the booming, bustling city of Seoul with its ten million inhabitants was like "climbing out of a deep, dark well." She met students at the Center from almost every country of Asia. The course work was an even greater challenge for her than nursing school had been. There were fat books to read in English, and papers to prepare and then present. Though she had been given a generous scholarship, Pema again had to work on the side to cover her expenses. But she kept at it with every ounce of strength she had and was able to successfully complete the course and get her degree.

Korea brought its own trials as well. Pema was in constant financial straits, having just barely enough to get along. She had an aversion to asking anyone for help. The Tibetans have a saying: "You run on what you have." Also, making known a financial need revealed one's social status; it was demeaning. So Pema preferred to scrape along on her own.

When the three years were up and it was time to return to Kathmandu, Pema had no money for a ticket. That had not been included in the scholarship package. So Pema lived in the ACTS guest house for two additional months, waiting for something to happen. Toward the end of that period Pema met two Korean Christian ladies who offered to help her with her airfare, but it was still not enough to cover the cost. So one of the ladies told Pema to pray, and so that night Pema prayed. The next day a letter addressed in her name arrived from Iceland with a check inside for the remaining amount needed to buy her plane ticket. Pema knew no one from Iceland; the name on the check was unknown to her. The following week she returned to Nepal.

In Kathmandu Pema began working with a dynamic Nepali Christian couple who had started a new church not far from the palace of the king of Nepal. That work grew rapidly, and within a few years it had become a network of several dozen churches. They started a Bible school, and Pema became one of the chief teachers. But this ministry mainly targeted Nepalis, not Tibetans. So after several years, Pema began to step out into a ministry that focused on Tibetans, many thousands of whom were now living in Nepal as refugees. This new ministry began to consume more and more of her time. As she mixed with the different Tibetan communities in Kathmandu and elsewhere in Nepal, she found a considerable number of Tibetans who had once professed faith in Christ but had later fallen away. The Tibetan believers lacked fellowship, teaching, and encouragement—the same lacks Pema herself had experienced in the years following nursing school. Isolated Tibetan Christians would attend Nepali churches, but they always felt out of place, uncomfortable. What they needed was a truly Tibetan fellowship where they could share with each other, come to trust each other, and build each other up in the faith.

So in 1994, Pema, the homeless, wandering, perpetual refugee, helped start a Tibetan Prayer Fellowship in Nepal, which was designed to provide a spiritual family for the struggling and isolated Tibetan Christians. Only Tibetans were invited. The first meeting was an enormous success and lasted for two days with twenty-two in attendance. The second meeting drew forty-five. And today these prayer fellowship meetings continue taking place several times each year in different parts of Nepal, providing great spiritual benefit to those who attend.

Ministry to Tibetans requires patience and persistence. Pema says the only way to be successful is by reaching down to the level of the people one is witnessing to. Evangelistic messages and preaching from pulpits are much less effective. Tibetan Buddhism is one of the most self-contained religious systems in the world; it is very hard to crack it open from the outside. Rather, slow and quiet identification with the people and coming alongside them as equals will yield more fruit. And the spiritual warfare that one will experience is intense, as Pema knows only too well. Even in the course of organizing her two-day prayer fellowship meetings, Pema has encountered many kinds of obstacles: city-wide strikes, closure of essential services, miscommunication, sickness—all occurring just before or during her meetings. But the most difficult spiritual warfare is from within the group of Tibetan believers themselves; they are naturally suspicious of each other, untrusting; their faith is often shaky; the pull backward into their old beliefs is powerful.

Historically, the majority of Tibetan Christians have come to faith in part through exposure to Christian hostels and orphanages in the Indian subcontinent. Tens of thousands of Tibetans today are displaced persons, refugees, torn from their homes, their roots. Because children's work has been one of the few effective means of bringing Tibetans to enduring faith in Christ, Pema has now embarked on yet a new and strategic project, the starting of a children's home in an important city of the Indian subcontinent where thousands of Tibetans live as refugees and where there is at present little sustained Christian work among them. Pema first came to know about Christ in the mission home in Gorakhpur. Today she is seeking to share that same knowledge with Tibetan youngsters who are homeless and rootless, as she once was.

OVERLAND—KATHMANDU TO LHASA

CHAPTER FIVE

To the north of Nepal lies forbidden, mysterious Tibet, the heart and center of Tibetan Buddhism. For over twenty years my wife Cynthia and I had looked up at the Himalayan peaks which mark the border between Nepal and Tibet, and looked forward to the day when we could cross over to the Tibetan side and see this land about which we had heard so much. The chance finally came in April, 1991, when Cynthia and I and our son Tom spent seven days in Tibet, with an eighth thrown in courtesy of C.A.A.C. (China Airlines Always Cancels), whose plane out was delayed a day because of bad weather.

The Chinese government had just opened Tibet to tourists, and one of the first tours offered was an overland journey in a small, well-traveled bus operated by a Nepali tour outfit. The tour was called, "Overland—Kathmandu to Lhasa in One Week." The return journey would be by plane and take one hour.

Kathmandu to Lhasa—two of earth's most exotic destinations, connected by a 600-mile dirt road winding over five passes above 15,000 feet. Perhaps one day they'll hold endurance races over that road, like the ones held each year across the Sahara. If they do, they'll need to offer a bigger prize.

In one sense we found everything as we had expected: the barren moonscape, broken by endless rows of jagged mountains; treeless stone villages separated by miles of desert; hundreds of ruined monasteries destroyed by the Chinese during the Cultural Revolution; dust, wind, and cold, not surprising in view of the journey's average altitude of 13,000 feet. And then, of course, there were the yaks; it's hard to imagine Tibet without her yaks. It was a yak that carried the Dalai Lama to safety in 1959, hours ahead of pursuing Chinese soldiers. That year

43

100,000 Tibetans lost their lives, and another 100,000 fled into exile in Nepal and India. Since then it is estimated that another million Tibetans have died under the harsh Chinese occupation.

The Tibetans we saw along the way we felt we already knew; we had met them in Nepal. At least five percent of Nepal's population is ethnically Tibetan. We'd had many patients who had trekked down from the Tibetan border to be treated at our mission hospital. And our first Nepal-trained nurse, Pasang Lama, was herself a Tibetan. In addition, there were the thousands of Tibetan refugees clustered in camps in and around Kathmandu and other cities of Nepal.

And yet, in another sense, Tibet was more impressive than we had imagined. From the five mountain passes we could sense the vastness of the land stretched out before us, an area the size of Texas, New Mexico and Arizona combined. There was a stark grandeur to the landscape. At the same time we found it desolate and intimidating. That two million Tibetans could scratch out their livelihood from this unforgiving environment is testimony to their fortitude and spirit.

The road to Lhasa runs east from Kathmandu and descends into the valley of the Sun Kosi River, elevation 1,500 feet. From there the road turns north, and begins a fifty-mile climb to 15,500 feet. Initially we followed the river valley, which soon turned into a precipitous gorge intersecting the main Himalayan range. Partway up the gorge we crossed the Tibetan border, and enjoyed our first night in a Chinese hotel, billed euphemistically in the guide book as "notoriously inefficient." Most memorable was the cracked toilet seat, which did not announce its intentions until one attempted to rise, at which point it bit into one's flesh like a giant crab. The hotel also housed the town's only disco, and it being Saturday night, the place was packed with young Chinese (not Tibetan) government employees, dancing mainly boy with boy, and girl with girl, but enjoying it nonetheless.

The second morning, as we ascended to the first pass, we were treated to magnificent views of the Himalayas—now, at last, seen from the north side. Near the top of the pass, our small bus broke down, giving us a few extra hours to gaze at the earth's mightiest mountain range strung out before us—and also to wonder what a night in that bus would be like at 15,000 feet. However, we eventually got under way again, and at the top of the pass we had our first unimpeded view of the interior of Tibet, the "roof of the world"—as well as the beginnings of altitude sickness. We then descended to 14,000 feet, where we were to spend the night in a newly opened tourist hotel.

The facility looked more like a prison than a hotel, which wasn't so odd, since we looked a lot like prisoners ourselves by that time, covered with dust, and apathetic from the high altitude. Everyone's first thought was a shower, but this hotel had no running water, which was a good thing in our room since the toilet reservoir had an inch-wide crack all the way down its front. It hadn't survived the overland journey from China, but had been installed all the same. Many of our party spent the night just trying to catch their breath, or being sick, or both. Actually, it is quite a marvel that a hotel should exist at all in such a remote and hostile place. It indicates the lengths to which the Chinese have gone to attract tourists to Tibet.

The third day was less rewarding, a ten-hour bus ride through a nearly continuous dust storm. This was the windy season in Tibet. The already bleak terrain was made more bleak by the swirling dust, so thick at times that we had to slow to a crawl just to stay on the road. If it was this unpleasant to drive through for just one day, what would it be like to live in such a place the year round?

We were a none-too-lively party that day. Three Italians among us had been told that chewing raw garlic was a good antidote for altitude sickness. I don't know what it did for them, but I know what it did for the rest of the bus. The arrival that evening at Tibet's second largest city, Xigaze, and at a respectable hotel was one of the most welcome moments of the trip.

Xigaze is famous for the Tashilhunpo Monastery, one of a handful that the Chinese left standing out of the hundreds that existed before 1960. After their vain attempt to eradicate the Tibetan Buddhist culture, the Chinese have now allowed the remaining monasteries to reopen. Over the past several years the number of monks has been steadily increasing. Ordinary Tibetans come in streams to worship at these monasteries, unmolested by the Chinese soldiers who everywhere stand passively on duty.

What the Chinese did to Tibet, of course, was terribly wrong, as evil as the rape of Kuwait by Iraq. At the same time, however, the Tibetan Buddhist monastic system was in itself a kind of "oppressor" of the people. Before the Chinese came, up to a quarter of the entire male population of Tibet lived in monasteries, supported by the rest of the populace. True, most monks worked hard and lived simply and provided various religious services, but they lived well above the level of the common people. They were a privileged class, and as such did not fit in with the ideals of the Cultural Revolution.

The next afternoon brought us a short two-hour drive to Gyangze, site of another large monastery and a fabulous castle perched high on a steep, rocky promontory. This latter structure reminded us of the castles depicted in illustrated story books of Europe in the Middle Ages. That evening the more venturesome of our party ate in a little roadside eatery, surrounded by runny-nosed Tibetan youngsters who descended on the uneaten food like vultures, scraping it into plastic bags to take home for their evening meal. The occasion was further enlivened by a patron at the next table who appeared to have gotten some phlegm stuck in his throat. His noises and contortions were so prolonged and violent that I thought he might deposit one of his lungs on the floor of the restaurant. We subsequently learned that this is quite acceptable behavior, comparable in the Middle East to a good hearty belch after dinner—the louder and longer the better.

The fifth day, the drive to Lhasa took us past 22,000-foot glacier-covered peaks, beautiful lakes, over a final breathtaking pass, and down into the valley of the Brahmaputra River. Then, an hour's drive up the Lhasa Valley and we were greeted by the familiar logo of Holiday Inn USA. It was peculiar that we, being Americans, should be spending our first night ever in a Holiday Inn—in Lhasa.

Lhasa's premiere attraction, of course, is the Potala, the palace of the Dalai Lamas. In spite of all the dramatic photos and tourist posters one has previously seen, the Potala itself does not disappoint. It opens twice a week for tourists and pilgrims, and one can wander for hours from top to bottom through its thousand rooms. Only the Dalai Lama's bedroom was off limits, it seemed. From the top, one gets a panoramic view of Lhasa, and it becomes apparent to what extent the old Tibetan section has been dwarfed and surrounded by the new Chinese part of the city. By the time the five-hour tour is finished, one's mind is numbed by the multitude of images and statues of various Buddhas and past Dalai Lamas, the numbness aggravated no doubt by the smoke from thousands of yak-butter candles, which are resupplied by the long lines of devotees pushing their way through the myriad rooms and alcoves.

The second main attraction in Lhasa is the ancient Jokhang Temple in the old city. At the entrance to the temple, one of the most sacred shrines in Tibet, dozens of worshipers repetitively prostrate themselves on the ground. Out in front there is a large open square where Tibetans in past years have demonstrated against the Chinese, and have been shot for their trouble. On the rooftops surrounding this square, Chinese sentries armed with machine guns stand guard, watching for any sign of unrest.

Outwardly the Tibetans themselves appear remarkably cheerful. When you meet them on the street their smiles are broad and their faces good-natured. At worship, however, they display little joy. They seem intent on the proper execution of their religious observances. It was hard to tell what, if any, solace, hope, or inspiration they received from the hundreds of different statues they bowed before. But it would have been hard to tell in any case; not only was there the language barrier, but even those few Tibetans who could speak English were afraid to talk to us—except for the ladies who tried to sell us trinkets.

On our last afternoon in Lhasa, Cynthia went shopping, and Tom and I visited Norbulingka, the great walled park in which the summer palaces of past Dalai Lamas are located. The park grounds are extensive, many city blocks square. The gardens have obviously deteriorated since the flight of the current Dalai Lama, though we saw a number of gardeners busy at work on this particular afternoon. The grounds contained several palaces, and the various gardens were separated by high walls. Most of the doorways through these walls were locked, but finding one door open, we went through into a particularly beautiful area, and sat down to enjoy the many flowering trees, which at that time were in full bloom.

Suddenly a harsh voice behind us said in English, "What are you doing in here?" A young man had come in behind us. We had evidently wandered into a section closed to visitors. But when we smiled and told him the door had been open, his manner softened, and he sat down and chatted with us. We soon got onto the subject of religion, and he seemed genuinely interested in what we had to say. We asked him where he had learned his English, and he told us he had an American teacher in Lhasa, working with the English Language Institute, China.

In such ways does the light flicker in this land. The number of true believers in Tibet proper is unknown, but it can probably be counted on one's fingers and toes. Teaching English is one of the greatest means of befriending Tibetans and opening their minds to the outside world. But it is not an easy task. Informal contact between student and teacher is strictly limited. The foreign teachers remain isolated not only from their students but also from each other; their movements and contacts are closely monitored. Nevertheless, the opportunities to witness do arise, and with the Spirit's help, fruit results. But more workers are needed; the harvest field is waiting.

The Lhasa airport is ninety miles south of the city, and situated along the Brahmaputra River. It is necessary to leave Lhasa at 6:00 a.m. in order to catch the 10:00 a.m. flight. On this day, after waiting in the terminal building until noon, we were informed that the flight had been canceled and that we would spend the night at the Airport Hotel, which turned out to be a few stars below the quality of the Holiday Inn. However, the television in the hotel room worked. That night I watched the Holyfield-Foreman heavyweight championship boxing match—live from Atlantic City, New Jersey. It's a global village indeed.

The flight from Lhasa back to Kathmandu surely has to be the most spectacular flight on earth. To the north, the unending mountain ranges of Tibet. To the south, the Himalayas. The plane passes between Kanchenjunga on the left (the world's third highest mountain), and Everest, Lhotse and Makalu on the right (the world's first, fourth and fifth highest mountains). The day we flew it was crystal clear. There were only about twenty-five passengers on our Boeing 707, so we could move back and forth from left to right, viewing the passing mountains from a variety of windows. The summits of the peaks were at eye level; every niche and ridge was etched with amazing sharpness. The flight was over much too soon, and before we knew it we were back to earth in Kathmandu.

Despite its inaccessibility and its sparse population, Tibet remains the spiritual nerve center of Tibetan Buddhism throughout the world, the place where the purest and most pervasive form of the religion is found. And Lhasa is the Mecca, the Jerusalem of Tibetan Buddhism. The might of the Chinese army has failed to conquer or even put a crack in the religious beliefs of the Tibetan people. Tibetan Buddhism remains today the most impenetrable religious system in the world.

A hundred years ago some Finnish missionaries established a mission center in Sikkim, just to the east of Nepal on the Tibetan border. Many times they attempted to enter Tibet but were prevented from doing so. One of those missionaries one day called out to the Lord, asking Him, "When is your time for Tibet?"

The Lord answered, "When my people rise up all along her border, then Tibet's time will come."

One hundred years ago there were no Christians anywhere along Tibet's border. Today Tibet is surrounded by Christians on the west, south, and east: two million in northern India, half a million in Nepal, tens of thousands in western China, and thousands in Sikkim. Tibet's time has now come.

A TIBETAN MONK COMES TO CHRIST

CHAPTER SIX

North of Xigaze, Tibet's second largest city, lies the township of Namling, site of the first of thirteen monasteries founded by the fifth Dalai Lama in the early 1600s. The monastery is called Ganden Chokhor, and it accommodates five hundred monks.

Nima Chothar was born into a farming family in a village just outside Namling in 1917. Nima's parents were tenant farmers; they worked for a powerful landowner and lived at his pleasure, much as serfs lived during the Middle Ages. Nima was the only son, and until he was six he lived at home with his parents and sisters. At home he used to play at being a monk; he would beat drums and perform sacred dances. This pleased his parents, and they encouraged him by giving him red and yellow clothing like the monks wore. It was an honor for one's son to become a monk, and so his parents hoped that when Nima was old enough he would enter the famous Ganden Chokhor monastery in nearby Namling.

When Nima was almost seven, his parents went to the landowner to ask permission for their son to become a monk. Since his parents were under the complete authority of the landowner, little Nima was also. Only with the landowner's permission could Nima escape a life of servitude on the farm and become a monk. The landowner granted the parents' request. The parents rejoiced at this, because now favor would shine on their family. Monks in Tibet were the elite of the land; they wielded great influence and enjoyed the esteem of the people. Back in those days a quarter of the male population of Tibet lived in monasteries and were supported by the rest of the populace.

There were hundreds of monasteries throughout Tibet, and similar to universities in the West, some monasteries were more prestigious than others. The Ganden Chokhor monastery was one of the most prestigious monasteries in all of Tibet, and many of the monks who were trained there went on later to become leading monks in Lhasa itself.

Nima's uncle happened to be a monk in Ganden Chokhor. So Nima's parents took him to see his uncle and to enlist the uncle's help in getting Nima enrolled in the monastery as a novice monk. The uncle agreed. But he said to Nima, "You must say you are seven years old. If you don't, you won't be allowed to stay in the monastery." The uncle then took Nima to see the abbot.

The abbot, dressed in his great robes and special hat, said to Nima, "I have three questions to ask you. First, are you the son of a blacksmith?"

"No, sir," said Nima.

"Are you the son of a butcher?"

"No, sir."

"Are you seven years old?"

"No, sir, I am only six. But my uncle told me to say I was seven."

Nima's uncle turned bright red, but the abbot laughed and said, "Since you have spoken truthfully you are worthy to become a monk. In the future you will be an honest man." And the abbot admitted Nima to the monastery as a novice monk.

Nima was one of sixty novice monks at Ganden Chokhor. From age eight to eleven, all the novices were required to study Tibetan. In addition, Nima studied Buddhist philosophy and a book called *Guide to the Bodhisattva's Way of Life*. At the end of the three years all sixty boys had to take an examination, and Nima came in first. For first prize, he was given a Tibetan ceremonial scarf.

Though Nima was a good student, he frequently got into trouble. He and a few friends would periodically escape from the monastery, but always they were caught by their parents and returned to the principal, who would have them punished. One time, Nima and two friends ran away and climbed to the top of a high mountain, where they stayed until they ran out of food. They even resorted to eating raw the eggs of some of the mountain birds who had built nests near the summit. Finally, overcome by hunger, they came down from the mountaintop and were promptly caught by their parents and returned to the monastery, where they were soundly whipped. Seeing that his uncle would no longer protect him, Nima drew apart from him, and began to devote himself to the further study of Buddhist philosophy.

When Nima was about fifteen, he asked his parents for permission to go to Lhasa, a nine-day journey by horse and mule. His parents gave their permission. When Nima reached Lhasa, he stayed in one of the colleges attached to the famous Sera Monastery, where about thirty monks from Ganden Chokhor were studying. Nima stayed at that college for two years, studying Buddhist scriptures and commentaries.

Then Nima returned to Namling and stayed with his friends from Ganden Chokhor and with his parents for half a year, during which time he made preparations for a more permanent move to Lhasa. Again the journey one way from Namling to Lhasa took nine arduous days of traveling by horse and mule over the barren mountainscape of central Tibet.

When Nima arrived back in Lhasa, he didn't stay at the Sera Monastery, but roomed instead with a friend of his in another section of Lhasa. During this period he did not wear the monk's robes, but dressed in ordinary clothes. When word of this reached his home in Namling, people there thought he had abandoned his monastic vows. But in his own view, he had not broken them; he still considered himself a monk.

At that time Nima became acquainted with a monk from the Dalai Lama's personal monastery in the Potala Palace. This monk said to Nima, "If you want to enter the Dalai Lama's monastery, I'll help you." With that encouragement, Nima began to set his sights on entering the Potala as one of the Dalai Lama's personal monks. This was one of the highest honors a monk could hope for. The Potala monks wore the best clothes, they were respected by all other monks, and they met frequently with the Dalai Lama.

However, before a new monk could enter the Dalai Lama's monastery, another monk of that monastery first had to die. And no monk seemed ready to die during that period to let Nima in. So after waiting for many months, Nima decided to enter another of Lhasa's well-known monasteries, the Drepung Monastery.

During Nima's futile wait to enter the Potala, he had arranged to have special clothes made for himself which would be suitable attire for the Dalai Lama's service. He was therefore wearing this attire when he first went to the Drepung Monastery. Consequently, the monks there thought he had come from the Potala itself, and hence accorded him great respect. This pleased Nima, for he was proud and enjoyed the homage paid to him.

When Nima asked to enter the Drepung Monastery, the monks there were happy to receive him, as they still thought he was a high-ranking monk of the Dalai Lama. One of the chief monks at Drepung agreed to be his special teacher. But he also said, "Entering this monastery will cost you a lot of money. However, I will help you by giving you some of my own money."

Between Nima's own money and that of his new teacher, there was enough to purchase the necessary articles required for admittance to the monastery. Nima lived in a special residence within the monastery, where the most privileged monks lived. These monks did not have to do the ordinary work that younger monks did; they ate better than the others, they sat in the highest seats in the assembly, and they were greeted respectfully by everyone. This special treatment gratified Nima's pride. After a few months he was given his own private room, and soon he was living pretty much as he pleased.

Discipline was slack for these privileged monks, and Nima's conduct gradually deteriorated. At the Tibetan New Year holiday that year, he and some fellow monks gambled late into the night with dice, and Nima ended up losing all of his money and possessions.

Shortly after that, the annual three-week prayer festival, called the Monlam, was held in Lhasa, with twenty thousand monks in attendance. On this occasion monks came from all the monasteries in the vicinity of Lhasa, and during the festival they received a great deal of money and food as alms from the common people. Equipped with these newly acquired supplies, Nima and two friends decided not to return to Drepung Monastery but rather to go on an extensive pilgrimage to various holy sites in Tibet. Their journey was completely unauthorized; they left without the knowledge of anyone at the monastery.

First they walked three days to Samye, Tibet's first monastery. Then they trekked many days into the hinterlands of Tibet, visiting sacred mountains, famous monasteries, and holy shrines. They received alms and honor wherever they went. They bought various articles in one place and then sold them at a profit in another place. By the end of their eight-month pilgrimage, they were no poorer than when they had started.

When Nima and his companions returned to Drepung Monastery, they were welcomed warmly by their teachers and friends, but they were sternly rebuked by their superior monk. Nima sincerely apologized, and thereafter abided by the rules of the monastery and avoided the friends who had gotten him into trouble.

One of Nima's functions as a monk was to go to the homes of people who had just died and recite a text known as the "Bardo Thodol." Tibetans believe that when someone dies, his or her spirit wanders in an intermediate state called the "Bardo" before attaining rebirth. During this period the person's spirit is terrified by visions of angry gods. Through hearing this particular text, Tibetans believe that the dead person can be delivered from the terror of these visions. The name "Bardo Thodol" means "deliverance through hearing in the Bardo." Nima has written in his short autobiography, *A Tibetan Monk's Story*:

> When a monk conducts such ceremonies, he receives so much good food and money for his services that he doesn't need to do any other kind of work. Often young monks don't think about the needs of the sick and the dying, but only about the money they receive for doing this ceremony.

One day Nima's main teacher came to him and said, "The Dalai Lama's bodyguard at the Potala needs a servant. Will you go?"

Nima jumped at the chance, and was soon installed as a servant of one of the Dalai Lama's four bodyguards, in which capacity he served for about a year. He spent the winter in the Potala and the summer in the Dalai Lama's summer palace, the Norbulingka. Few people ever got to see the Dalai Lama in person, but the bodyguards and their servants saw him every day. At that time the Dalai Lama was about thirteen years old. Nima felt very important going here and there in the company of the Dalai Lama, and the particular bodyguard he served was good to him and gave him fine food to eat and rich clothes to wear.

Toward the end of that year with the Dalai Lama's bodyguard, word came from Nima's parents asking him to return home at once. They had again become fearful that Nima had broken his vows, because while serving the bodyguard he did not customarily wear monk's robes but rather ordinary clothing. When he arrived home, Nima assured his parents that he had not broken his vows; however, they were not happy to let him go back to Lhasa and continue with the body-guard. They urged him to join a monastery nearer to his home; and so Nima decided to join the famous Tashilhunpo Monastery in the nearby city of Xigaze. Tashilhunpo was the greatest monastery outside of Lhasa; it was founded by the first Dalai Lama in the early 1400s and had 3,800 monks. It was the seat of succession of the Panchen Lamas, and all Panchen Lamas were buried there. It would be a great honor to be a Tashilhunpo monk, so Nima was more than happy to oblige his parents by joining that monastery. In order to be admitted to full membership, Nima had to undergo six months of special spiritual training and then pass an exam.

Again Nima began to associate with some of the more undisciplined young monks, who spent much of their time gambling in the park outside the monastery grounds. These monks, Nima among them, often refused to fulfill their duties, and as a result they were whipped from time to time by the monk in charge of discipline. Tiring of this, Nima and two fellow monks again escaped from the monastery. They decided to leave Tibet altogether, and so they journeyed south to the country of Bhutan, where they were warmly welcomed by the Bhutanese people. The Bhutanese have great respect for monks coming from Tibet, and the three monks had no end of offers of places to stay. A number of families invited them to stay in their homes indefinitely and serve as "house lamas." So Nima and his friends stayed in Bhutan for a year, enjoying the abundant hospitality of the Bhutanese people without spending a penny of their own.

After a year in Bhutan, Nima decided to go on pilgrimage to India. He started out in April, but by the time he had reached Gangtok, the capital of Sikkim, it had become so hot that he could not continue. So he stayed in Gangtok and served as a house lama for a wealthy Sikkimese family, taking care of all the affairs of the household. This included carrying out religious observances, reciting scriptures, taking care of the children, shopping, and providing hospitality to guests. During this time Nima learned to speak Nepali and Hindi, the main languages of Sikkim. After nine months, Nima quit this service and resumed his pilgrimage to India.

During the next several years, Nima's wanderings took him to various Buddhist holy places across North India, back to Sikkim, and once back to his home in Tibet where he temporarily rejoined the

Tashilhunpo Monastery. But in 1950 his wanderlust again got the better of him, and he returned to Bhutan, where the people had treated him so royally on his first visit. He lived again with some of the families he had stayed with four years earlier.

During this second visit, Nima noticed that a fellow monk was living with a Bhutanese woman. He thought to himself, "I would never do that." But there is a Tibetan proverb which says: "Whatever you think you may or may not do, your fate will be determined by your deeds in your previous life." And so it wasn't long afterwards that during a festival commemorating the preaching of the Buddha's first sermon Nima and several fellow monks got drunk on *chang* (Tibetan beer) and broke their monastic vows by sleeping with Bhutanese women. The next day Nima felt sad and ashamed. He decided he couldn't stay in Bhutan any longer. In his own words, he "felt deep regret, but there was no way to repent and take it back. To have thought ahead would have been wise; to feel sorry about it later was stupid."

Nima recalled a proverb of the Buddha: "Chang is the root of all evil; never take even the smallest drop."

And a parable goes with it: "The devil went to tempt a monk to break his vows. He set before him a pot of chang, a goat, and a woman, and asked him, 'Will you drink the chang, or kill the goat, or commit immorality with the woman?' The monk thought, 'If I kill the goat, that's the sin of killing. If I take the woman, that's the sin of immorality. Perhaps I'll drink the chang.' He did so and became drunk, killed the goat, and defiled himself with the woman. There is no greater vice in the world than drinking chang."

So Nima left Bhutan and went to Pagri, just over the border in Tibet. There he got a high-paying job carrying loads of Tibetan wool across the Himalayas to Kalimpong, and then carrying kerosene back to Pagri. After doing this for a few months, Nima began working for a man in Kalimpong who baked bread and prepared Tibetan dumplings called "mo-mos." The man went out of business a year later, but by that time Nima had learned to cook. So he traveled to Calcutta and found a job as a cook. But the climate there was so hot he could barely eat, and he gradually lost his strength. Some months later he came down with malaria.

Tibetans, used to the cold, dry, high altitude of their native land, do not do well in the steamy, tropical cities of India. Unable to work,

Nima headed north for the Indian town of Baxaduars, located in the hill country near the India-Bhutan border. Many wealthy Bhutanese families lived there, and so Nima found some monk's clothes, put them on, and again took up his vocation as a monk, going from house to house reciting Buddhist scriptures in return for alms.

However, his malaria got worse, and he became dangerously ill. There was a Christian mission hospital in Baxaduars run by the Finnish Mission. A Finnish missionary, Miss Hellin Hukka, took care of Nima and nursed him back to health. Nima thought that the hospital people were very kind.

After he had recovered, Nima again began going out to recite Buddhist scriptures in the homes of the Bhutanese, for which he was generously recompensed with food and money. However, Miss Hukka encouraged him, instead, to enter her employment as a general caretaker and medical assistant; and so he did so, taking up residence in a small apartment near her home. He helped her with the many patients who came to the hospital, cleaning and bandaging their sores and rendering other services. Morning and evening he attended the mission worship services.

Miss Hukka gave Nima a Bible. In the Bible he read about how God created the earth, the heavens and the oceans, and all living objects found therein. He read how God created the first man and woman, and how they disobeyed God and became sinners, and how their sin was passed on to all who followed them.

"But," Nima writes in his autobiography, "according to our Buddhist religion, the world arose by itself. A monkey, the emanation of the god Chenresi, was the father of all men, and a rock-demon, the emanation of the goddess Dolma, was the mother of all men. That was the way mankind began. But the Christians taught that God had made everything. I had to think about which story was true. Even if that monkey could be the father of mankind, how could the rock-demoness be the mother?"

Then in the book of the prophet Isaiah Nima read that there is only one true God, that all other gods and idols are not God, and making sacrifices to them is pointless. They have eyes but they can't see, and ears but they can't hear. Nima thought: "How is that? If this is true, all the religion I've practiced so far is worthless. Surely this Christian religion is unsuitable for Tibetans." And he quit reading the Bible. However, morning and evening he continued attending the Christian worship services and acting as though he believed, for, as he says, "the Christians were taking care of me."

One day a pretty Bhutanese girl came to the hospital with a sore on her foot. She had been treated in Bhutan, but the sore had not healed. The sore smelled badly, and the girl was embarrassed to show it to Nima. But Nima reassured her, and gently took her foot and washed the sore and bandaged it. Daily the girl returned to the hospital to have Nima put on a clean dressing, and within a month the sore was healed. By that time, the girl and Nima had taken a liking to each other, and had decided to live together. However, before they could carry out their plan, Miss Hukka found out about it and sent the girl away to Darjeeling, an Indian hill town a two-day journey away. This upset Nima greatly, and he began to think these Christians were indeed nasty people who specialized in spoiling the happiness of others.

Nima immediately left for Darjeeling to hunt for his girlfriend. But as soon as he had departed, Miss Hukka telephoned Darjeeling and had the girl sent back again! Never underestimate the determination of single missionary women. When Nima found his girlfriend was not in Darjeeling, he was disconsolate. He found a local boarding house, put his things there, and then began to wander up and down the streets of the town. After a while he came to Darjeeling's central market, and there he met a tall Englishman named Ernest Shingler. The Englishman greeted him like an old friend and asked him what kind of work he was doing.

Nima said, "I don't have any work."

Mr. Shingler said, "I have some work for you to do. Are you interested?"

"What kind of work is that?" Nima asked.

"Teaching me and my wife Tibetan," Mr. Shingler answered.

Nima happily agreed, and Mr. Shingler found a small room near his house where Nima could stay. And thereafter, every day at 2:00 p.m. Nima would teach Mr. and Mrs. Shingler the Tibetan language. And, in turn, the Shinglers taught Nima more about Christianity.

Nima thought to himself, "When I left Miss Hukka, I swore I'd never believe in this Jesus religion. And now I'm hearing about it all over again. Maybe it's my fate to learn it." So Nima listened to what Mr. Shingler had to say, and even began to read the Bible again. Before long he began to forget about his Bhutanese girlfriend.

For many weeks Nima was torn between the claims of the Christian God and his old belief in the gods of Buddhism. He writes in his autobiography:

> Because I'd studied Buddhism for so many years, I couldn't leave it. Occasionally I still said mantras and recited texts; and I still believed in the Buddhist gods and idols. The Christians were very devout, but I wondered why they made no offerings to their God. "After all, it isn't a sin to make offerings," I thought.
>
> One day when I was reading the Bible's book of Isaiah, I found this written: "From one tree a man cuts a piece of wood, throws it in the fire and cooks his food. From another he makes an idol and bows down to it, praying to it, 'Save me!' But the idol doesn't answer and it cannot save." After reading that, my faith in the Buddhist gods grew less and less.

Not long afterward, Nima became ill with tuberculosis. With Mr. Shingler's help, he was admitted to a small government tuberculosis hospital, where he stayed for eleven months. Mr. Shingler would come to the hospital three times a week for his Tibetan language lessons. Each time, he would pray with Nima, and Nima was greatly encouraged and strengthened by these times of prayer.

While Nima was still in the hospital he took a correspondence course offered by the nearby Mirik Bible School. Through this, his understanding of the Christian faith deepened, and his way of thinking changed. He was able to quit many of his former bad habits.

One day a Pentecostal evangelist from South India visited the hospital. Through his prayers, a number of the patients were healed. Then the evangelist came to Nima and asked, "Do you believe in Jesus?"

Nima said, "I do."

Then the evangelist asked, "Do you believe that if you pray to Jesus your illness will get better?"

"I do," said Nima.

Then the evangelist put his hand on Nima's head and prayed for his healing in a loud voice. Then he left, saying that he'd be back the next day.

The next day the evangelist returned, and read to Nima from 2 Corinthians 6:2, where Paul writes: "'In the time of my favor I heard you, and in the day of salvation I helped you.' I tell you, now is the time of God's favor, now is the day of salvation."

The evangelist said to Nima, "It is written: '. . . by his wounds you have been healed.' Now your disease is healed. If you believe this, you have no more sickness, and you can go home." Nima felt that the disease had left his body, and he felt a great peace in his heart.

The next day when the doctor came in, Nima asked him for permission to leave the hospital. The doctor asked Nima why he wanted to leave before his treatment was finished. Nima said, "I know my disease is gone, and I want to go home." And over the objections of the doctor, Nima left the hospital. And his tuberculosis never returned.

Nima went immediately to tell Mr. and Mrs. Shingler what had happened, and they rejoiced with him. Over the next several weeks, many verses from the Bible took on new meaning for Nima, in particular Hebrews 10:22: ". . . let us draw near to God with a sincere heart in full assurance of faith, having our hearts sprinkled to cleanse us from a guilty conscience and having our bodies washed with pure water."

Nima describes his experience in these words: "After reading this (Heb. 10:22), I received a new heart. I turned away from my adultery, drinking, and other sins; and confessing them, left them all behind. All my sins were washed away in the blood of the Lord Jesus. Now I was a real Christian."

It had taken Nima three long years to finally and fully come to faith in Christ. Now he was ready to be baptized. His baptism took place in November, 1955, at the historic Finnish mission station in Ghoom, near Darjeeling. Nima writes:

> Because the weather was cold, the church people had poured a great deal of hot water into the place where I was to be baptized, but the air was so cold that this had little effect. My friends wanted to give me special help, for I was the first Tibetan they had baptized.

After his baptism, Nima thought he should look elsewhere to find work, so as not to leave the impression that he had been baptized merely in order to get a job. So he returned to his old employment in Calcutta, where four years earlier he had worked a short time before getting sick with malaria. If his old employer in Calcutta was amazed to see Nima restored to physical health, she was even more amazed to see the change in Nima's behavior. From a dissolute and hot-tempered brawler he had turned into a praying and Bible-reading gentleman.

With the arrival of summer Nima again had to leave the heat of Calcutta and return to the hills. But on the train north, all Nima's possessions were stolen. He was stranded in unfamiliar territory without a friend or any source of help. Having no money, he set out on foot to Darjeeling to find Mr. Shingler. After a journey of several days, he reached his destination and was warmly welcomed by his Christian acquaintances there. Mr. Shingler again tided Nima over until he could find a job.

Nima found work at a restaurant, where he soon became manager. A young Tibetan woman named Rigdzin was also working at the restaurant, and after a few months they fell in love and decided to get married. They were married in the restaurant in the summer of 1956.

Rigdzin was not a Christian. But after her marriage she received much teaching and encouragement from Nima, Mr. Shingler, and others, and by the following year she too believed in Christ and was baptized. Nima and Rigdzin then had a second wedding service, this time a Christian one.

Over the next two years Nima and Rigdzin became involved in various Christian ministries in the Darjeeling area. Then came 1959, when the Chinese invaded Tibet and thousands of Tibetan refugees escaped over the Himalayan mountain passes into Nepal and India. Many came to Darjeeling, and Nima and Rigdzin were able to offer these new arrivals much assistance.

They also witnessed to them. Once they brought a supply of Christian books to a large compound where many Tibetan refugees were staying. Some monks at the compound took the books. When Nima and his wife were leaving, a policeman stopped them and brought them to the police chief. Some of their books were there on his desk. One of the monks must have reported their activities to the police. The police chief asked, "Who sent you here with these books?"

Nima answered, "The Lord."

The police chief said, "Who is he? You two are to leave here and not come back, or I'll put you in prison."

When Nima and Rigdzin were on their way again, they met some of the monks who had received their books; they were hiding the books under their robes. "If you have any more like these, bring them tomorrow," they said. "We want to read them." Most of the monks desired to learn about Christianity, and this desire opened up many opportunities for Nima and Rigdzin to witness to them.

The numbers of Tibetan refugees continued to increase, and Nima and his wife were kept busy ministering to their physical and spiritual needs in the towns along the Tibetan border. Among the refugees were many children. So Nima, together with Thomas Patton, an English evangelist, started a school in a town on the Sikkim-India border where many Tibetan refugees had settled. The first year they had ten students and the second year, fifty. Because of the increasing number of students, they moved the school to the larger city of Kalimpong, where it was named Avila House. And there Nima and Rigdzin labored for the next ten years, teaching and nurturing young Tibetans. Out of twenty students who went on to college, eight have become Christians. During this time God also gave Nima and his wife a son, Yacob.

In 1968 Nima and Rigdzin were asked to serve as houseparents in a large Moravian mission school in Dehra Dun, a major city located in the Himalayan foothills in northwestern India. Though they believed that this was God's call to them, they had to overcome many obstacles before they actually began their work in Dehra Dun. At one point Nima was arrested for being a Tibetan Christian and thrown in prison with robbers and murderers. His case dragged on for three months, and at the end he was expelled from Dehra Dun. Wherever he went in North India, he was not allowed to stay. Finally his health broke down and he became severely ill. A kind official in the state capital, Lucknow, heard his story and had compassion on him, and granted him a residence permit to stay anywhere in the state—which included Dehra Dun. So finally, after many months of trial and delay, Nima and his wife started their work at the Moravian school in Dehra Dun, a work that continued for the next ten years.

In 1978 Nima was ordained as a pastor by the Moravian bishop in Lucknow, and he became the pastor of the Moravian church in Dehra Dun. He had never received formal theological training, but he had gained much spiritual understanding through his own experiences and through his contact with missionaries. Nima served in that church for four years. He baptized sixteen people and married twelve couples. But he says, "Thanks to God's grace, I didn't have to conduct any funerals."

In 1982 Nima and Rigdzin felt called to go to Nepal and minister to the ever-growing Tibetan refugee community in Kathmandu. There at the big mission hospital Nima met an American missionary doctor who also had a special burden for the Tibetan people. Many of the Tibetan refugees would come to the hospital in serious condition, not knowing the Nepali language or anyone who could help and advise them. Many had nowhere to stay after being discharged from the hospital. One Tibetan left the hospital, had nowhere to go, and died a few days later. When the American doctor heard about it, he determined to do something to help. So he and Nima started a home for poor and ill Tibetans in Kathmandu. They rented a large eight-room house and called it "Champacholing," which means, "the place of God's love." They opened the home in September, 1983, with Nima and Rigdzin supervising the work. Nima then started a small Tibetan carpet factory with twelve weavers, hoping thereby to make Champacholing self-sufficient and to provide employment for patients staying at the home. And after a few years Nima started a children's home, which today houses twenty-five Tibetan children. And Nima continues to serve as pastor of a slowly growing Tibetan church in Kathmandu. His son Yacob, after studying theology in Korea, has joined him in the work.

I last met Pastor Nima in April, 1996, on the top-floor chapel of his children's home, a four-story, brick-and-cement building in the crowded center of Kathmandu. It was the weekly Sunday afternoon service, and twenty-five Tibetan youngsters sat cross-legged on the floor listening solemnly to Pastor Nima's sermon. At eighty, the fire and sparkle had diminished somewhat, but Nima was still able to keep the attention of his audience throughout his forty-five-minute message. He spoke slowly and with feeling. He told his listeners that the Christian life involved much suffering; it was like a pilgrimage through strange and alien lands. One could see in his eyes that he knew what he was talking about.

DAVID TSERING

CHAPTER SEVEN

High in the western Himalayas bordering Tibet lies the Indian state of Ladakh and its capital city, Leh. On Ladakh's northern border, the world's second-highest mountain, Godwin Austin (K2), crowns the Karakoram Range, its mighty summit falling away in great curved rivers of ice which flow down between the lesser peaks. This remote mountainous region is home to many thousands of Tibetans, who fled across the border into India during the 1959 annexation of their homeland by the Chinese. The majority of these refugees had been people of education and influence in their former country; many of them were monks, or lamas. In Ladakh they have built monasteries and schools for the equipping of the next generation of Tibetans, on whom it will fall to preserve and perpetuate the Tibetan Buddhist culture. More than anywhere else today, Ladakh constitutes the center of influence of Tibetan Buddhism. Just nearby in the state of Himal Pradesh, the Dalai Lama himself has his residence-in-exile.

On a summer night in 1989, a handsome young Tibetan man was walking along the streets of Leh toward the Christian church which he was pastoring. A Muslim friend came running up to him and said, "Get inside your house quickly. They are coming to kill you." Pastor David Tsering didn't wait to question his friend; he knew it was true. That very night hundreds of the leading lamas had been meeting together. The meeting had just broken up and the lamas, dressed in their long yellow robes, were heading for the church, shouting angrily as they marched. They held aloft hastily made placards proclaiming, "Death to the pastor." Other Tibetans came out of their houses and joined the procession. David Tsering hurried down the winding back streets to his home, motioned to his wife to be silent, and bolted the doors. The church was nearby. David and his wife could hear the ever-increasing commotion of the crowd, as the people gathered in the square near the church. All night long the lamas and the crowd chanted and shouted. By morning over four thousand Tibetans had congregated to denounce the pastor and his church. The lamas circulated a pamphlet entitled, *Our Religion is in Danger*, which warned that Tibetan Buddhism was under insidious attack by a handful of turncoats in their midst. Word of this peril spread that day throughout all of Leh, and by the next morning the crowd had grown to twelve thousand stomping, shouting, placard-waving Buddhists. Hidden in their house, Pastor David and his wife were on their knees pleading with God that they and their church might be delivered from the angry mob outside.

How did this gentle and unassuming man bring such wrath upon his head? David's story begins forty years earlier in the Tibetan city of Amdo, two hundred miles north of Lhasa, where his father was the second-ranking monk at Amdo Monastery. In the early 1950s the Chinese army began to mass along the Tibetan border, and increasingly strident propaganda circulated throughout Tibet calling for the abolition of Tibet's monastic system and the arrest of its religious leaders. Sensing the danger, David's father left Amdo on a pilgrimage to the south, and he ended up near the border of Bhutan, where he settled. There he met a young woman—who would become David's mother—and decided to marry her, even though it meant leaving his monastic life behind.

David was born there in southern Tibet in 1953, the second of three sons. It being the tradition among Tibetans that one of a family's sons should be dedicated to become a monk, David's father selected him to receive the honor. Accordingly, from a young age David began to study the Tibetan language and the Buddhist religion.

In 1959, with the Chinese occupation of Tibet nearly complete, David's father was forced to flee with his family to Kalimpong in India, a large town to the east of Nepal, where many other Tibetans had found refuge. A very prominent Rinpoche, or leading monk, had also fled to Kalimpong, and David's father wanted his son to be trained by this man. So David became a disciple of this eminent Rinpoche, and continued his study of the Tibetan language and religion.

During this period, David experienced a growing hunger to know God, to know the truth. He did not feel a freedom in his studies to search for the truth, wherever that search might lead. What he learned he learned under compulsion. Hence he did not truly believe the teaching of the Rinpoche; his assent was forced. Furthermore, what he was learning just did not ring true. There was something lacking. The Rinpoche's teaching failed to explain the meaning and purpose of life; it did not impart wisdom. Whenever David questioned something, the Rinpoche's answer was always, "You don't need to understand; you're not supposed to understand." And so David did not find answers; he was just told to believe. He was frustrated and dissatisfied. Reflecting on this years later, David asks: "What is the appeal of Tibetan Buddhism to Westerners? Why do they follow such a religion?"

During this period of study with the Rinpoche, David's family suffered much economic hardship. Although they had been well-off in Tibet, now as refugees they were poor. Because of this, when a home for needy Tibetan boys was opened a year or so after their arrival in Kalimpong, David's father decided to place him and his brothers in this home. This home was established by the English missionary, Thomas Patton, mentioned in the previous chapter. David's father had perhaps not reckoned on the possible spiritual impact this home might have on his son; or if he had, he must have concluded that the financial benefit outweighed the spiritual risk.

David was about ten years old when he entered Tom Patton's home. Patton had also started a school for the Tibetan boys living in the home. Among the teachers was an ethnic Nepali pastor, Robert Mukhya, who lived outside Kalimpong. Robert used to walk three miles to and from his house each day to teach the boys in Patton's school. His subject was the Bible. David remembers him being filled with joy. He was so good-natured; he sang and joked as he taught. His eyesight was failing, but he never complained. He related the Bible to his personal life; he made it alive and meaningful. He also taught the boys English. Pastor Robert went blind before he died; but he left a mark on his students that would never be erased.

For David and his fellow students, Pastor Robert was a new kind of teacher. Under the Rinpoche, David had been taught by rote. He had been required to memorize and memorize, but what he was memorizing was never explained or applied. With Robert it was different; whatever Robert taught he applied to his students' lives.

Memory is, of course, a great gift, and it is enhanced with practice. David continued to use his memory; in particular, he began memorizing passages from the Bible. As God's Word more and more filled his mind, the former Buddhist teachings were, in David's words, "flushed away." But this did not happen quickly. For many years those Buddhist teachings had dominated his thinking and his behavior; it would take time for the new teaching to overcome the old.

One of Robert's major contributions to David's thinking concerned idols. According to the teaching of the Rinpoche, idols were considered to be actual gods. But according to Robert, idols were simply objects made of mud or stone. Idols didn't breathe, speak, or even move. Robert didn't criticize Buddhism or any other belief system; he merely stated the facts and let his students draw their own conclusions.

David continued at Tom Patton's school in Kalimpong all the way through high school. But he never truly adopted the Christian religion as his own; he never had a personal experience of faith, a personal encounter with God. But in his last years in the school, he met an Australian evangelist, Don Stanton, who was the publisher of a magazine called *Christian Challenge*. Don Stanton needed a proofreader for his magazine, and when he discovered that David had become proficient in English under the tutelage of Pastor Robert, he asked David to help him do some of the proofreading. It was through this proofreading during his final year in high school, that David felt personally called by God; it was God's Word itself that called him. And the one verse more than any other that spoke to David's heart was John 15:16: "You did not choose me, but I chose you and appointed you to go and bear fruit—fruit that will last."

When David related this to me during our interview together for the writing of this chapter, I thought back to my own experience, for it had been that same verse that God had used more than any other to call me to missionary service. Yet for David it had not been God's Word all by itself, out of the blue. That word had been sown in David's heart. It had been sown by a sower—several, in fact: Tom Patton, Pastor Robert, Don Stanton. David had needed to see that the Word of God really made a difference in these men's lives, and then his own heart needed to be open and ready to receive that word. And in God's time, that seed sprouted and took root, and it has been bearing fruit ever since.

Don Stanton was based in Simla, a hill town in North India to the west of Nepal. Himachal University is located there, and Don helped David get admitted to that university, and helped with his tuition and expenses. In return, David continued to do proofreading for Don's magazine.

David graduated from university in 1973, and got a job teaching at the Moravian mission school in Dehra Dun, the same school where Nima Chothar and his wife Rigdzin once served as houseparents. During his first year there, David again experienced the personal call of Jesus—this time stronger than ever before. One day Jesus' words again came back to him: "You did not choose me, but I chose you and appointed you. . . ." And David realized that he had not yet fully and unreservedly responded to that call, that appointment. And that day he knelt down in his room and gave his life to Jesus.

Shortly thereafter, the director of the school, an ordained minister, baptized David. And the following year, David married the director's daughter. The blessing of the Lord came more quickly than David had ever imagined!

A year later David was accepted at Canadian Theological Seminary in Regina, Saskatchewan, where he completed a master's degree in Religious Education. He then served as an interim pastor in a Moravian church in Edmonton, Alberta, as part of the seminary's internship program. At the end of that time he was ordained as a Moravian church pastor.

When David returned to India in 1978, he pastored a Moravian church in the Indian city of Rajpur, and he also was principal of a Moravian school there. Then in 1980, God called David to serve as pastor in the city of Leh, the capital of Ladakh, a place where he would serve for almost ten years.

Leh is an old city located just north of the broad valley of the upper Indus River, 11,000 feet in elevation. Surrounded on three sides by 24,000-foot mountains, it lies on an ancient trade route linking India and western China. Its narrow streets wind between high, whitewashed walls. In the center of town is the square, a broad area surrounded by shops, and large enough to accommodate a crowd of twelve thousand angry Buddhists.

Though a small minority of the population is Muslim, most of the residents of Leh are Tibetan Buddhists, their numbers swollen by the influx of Tibetans fleeing from the Chinese invaders. A century earlier, German Moravians had arrived in Leh and opened a mission station near the square in the center of town; eventually they established a church. It was this Moravian church to which David had been called to serve as pastor.

When David arrived in 1980, there were no more than a handful of baptized believers within the Tibetan community. Patiently and diligently David applied himself to the work of ministry. He visited the sick, he comforted the sorrowing, he presented the gospel to all who would listen. His own small flock he tended with care, teaching them, admonishing them, encouraging them. His church grew. By 1989, there were seventy baptized believers, and weekly attendance at church services had reached one hundred and fifty. At that time, the only other Tibetan congregations in the world were those led by Nima Chothar and Eva Schmidt, and David's was the largest and best established of the three.

Then in 1989 David wrote a small book in Tibetan called *The Savior*. It consisted of eighty-three devotional lessons on the life and ministry of Jesus Christ. The book was instantly popular; Tibetans eagerly sought for copies. David had ordered a printing of two thousand, most of which were kept in his storeroom. He had wondered how he would ever get rid of them all, but they were gone in no time. Another three thousand copies arrived. The youth from his church began to distribute them. David himself journeyed all over Ladakh, all along the Chinese border, preaching, teaching, and making his book available. All five thousand books were sold—and then the trouble began.

Here is David's version of events. The Tibetan hierarchy, the lamas, correctly perceived that David's book was a threat to their power and authority. Therefore, the leading lamas in Leh made three decrees: first, David was to be expelled from Ladakh; second, his book was to be banned; and third, all further conversions were to be forbidden.

As these decrees were announced to the inhabitants of Leh, the entire city rose up against David. This was the day when the twelve thousand Buddhists gathered in the square. God restrained them from doing violence to David at that time; David and his wife remained safely in their house. The crowd eventually dispersed—though not for long. Within days the Buddhists were demonstrating again. The continuing threats of violence and the angry public meetings so alarmed the Indian government officials that they clapped a curfew on the city that ended up lasting three months. The government also gave David a bodyguard of seventeen policemen to protect him and the church property from harm.

The actions of the Indian government officials infuriated the lamas and the rest of the citizens of Leh. In their minds the provocateurs were no longer the Christians alone but the Indian authorities as well. The Buddhist community rose up in protest against the government. The more radical elements resorted to violence, which resulted in shootings and deaths. The Buddhists themselves became divided over tactics: some wanted to fight only David and the Christians; others wanted to fight the Indian government in hopes of gaining greater autonomy for their people. Soon Buddhists were attacking Buddhists. To David, they behaved much like the workers on the tower of Babel who lost the ability to communicate intelligently with one another.

At one point during the protracted confusion, David sneaked out of Leh and went to Delhi, the Indian capital, to ask for protection for minority rights. India, being a secular democracy, is committed to upholding the rights of all of its citizens. As the turmoil showed no sign of abating, the Indian Prime Minister, Rajiv Ghandi, instructed Ladakh's Chief Minister to go to Leh and "solve the matter." The uprising had already lasted three months.

When the Chief Minister learned that the cause of the trouble had been David's book, he asked that an English translation of the book be sent to him at once. So the book was translated overnight from Tibetan into English, and the manuscript was sent to the Minister the very next day by helicopter. Finding the book to be insufficient cause for such an uprising, the Minister severely reprimanded the Buddhist leaders for inciting their followers and threatened them with imprisonment if they continued their rebellion. After that, an uneasy peace settled on the city.

During the three months of turmoil, the members of David's congregation had gradually begun to fall away. The unbaptized attenders were the first to go. But to David's dismay, the baptized believers also, one by one, ceased coming to the church. When David confronted them individually and asked them why they had left, they would say, "We have enough difficulties of our own. You wrote the book that caused all this trouble; it's your problem, not ours. We have families to care for.

Our relatives say it is because we were Christians that we have suffered this way. We cannot continue with you any longer."

By the time peace finally came, not one of David's congregation stood with him; only his wife remained by his side. He recalled the similar situation which had faced the Apostle Paul, when, in Paul's words, ". . . No one came to my support, but everyone deserted me" (2 Tim. 4:16). To see one's labor of ten years evaporate into nothing would have overcome a lesser man, but David found his faith strangely strengthened. He was cast upon Christ in a way he had never been before; he learned to lean on Him, to trust Him. David, looking back, says now that that crisis was the "highlight" of his ministry.

Not long after the uprising had subsided, David and his wife left Leh and moved to Mussoorie, an Indian hill town north of Delhi. There in 1990 he became the leader of a new ministry—this time a radio ministry called "Gaweylon," which in Tibetan means, "Good News." This ministry produces its own Tibetan materials and has its own studio, and its broadcasts are beamed into Tibet from a large transmitter located on an island in the Indian Ocean. One of the materials broadcast is a little book of eighty-three devotional lessons by David Tsering called *The Savior.*

I first met David Tsering in 1991 in the very center of Tibet. He was traveling from east to west, and I was traveling west to east. We met outside the Tashilhunpo Monastery in Xigaze, Tibet's second largest city. I asked him how many Tibetan Christians he thought there were inside Tibet. Holding up his outstretched fingers, he replied, "Inside Tibet I doubt there are more than ten. Outside Tibet I cannot say, but I'm sure the number is very small."

David told me about the radio ministry he was just then getting involved in. He said that radio programs in Tibetan had been coming into the country for decades, but as yet there had been virtually no discernible fruit. David said, "Without flesh-and-blood missionaries here on the ground to reinforce and embody the radio message, radio ministry alone can never win this country for Christ. People need to physically see the messenger, the witness, before they can be convinced that the message is really for them."

David was right. Radio and literature and other ancillary means of communicating the gospel are vital, but in the absence of missionaries they cannot win a nation to Christ. No new ground has ever been gained, no church among an unreached people has ever been established in the absence of a living witness, a missionary. So it has always been. God's instruments of choice for reaching the nations are missionaries. David is such a missionary—both on the air and on the ground.

Meanwhile, back in Leh, Ladakh, a new pastor leads the little Moravian church. In the summer of 1996, a three-day evangelistic crusade was held there, and thirty-five Tibetan Buddhists accepted Christ. The groundwork laid by those first Moravians, and later by David Tsering, continues to bear fruit. We need to pray that it will last.

A HIGH PRICE PAID

CHAPTER EIGHT

Nestled high in the Himalayan Mountains is a little-known principality which is home to half a million Tibetan Buddhists. The rulers of this principality have not been eager to have foreigners working in their land, especially foreign Christians. Yet the land is poor and undeveloped. Health standards are low, tuberculosis and leprosy are endemic, and malnutrition is common. Some years ago a handful of Christian health workers were allowed into the country to help meet the people's pressing medical needs. Among them were a Scottish doctor named Bruce Macauley and his Irish wife Hilda, a psychologist turned teacher. They arrived in the country in 1980, and Bruce took on the job of medical superintendent of a mission hospital in a remote town in the eastern part of the country. He was also appointed District Medical Officer of the Royal Government, which meant being responsible for thirty thousand people spread out over an area of 1,500 square miles of rugged mountains. Only a few years earlier the only responsibility Bruce had ever wanted was responsibility for himself.

Bruce was a long time getting to the place where God wanted him. He had grown up as one of seven children in a middle-class neighborhood in Scotland. As a child he had accepted the faith handed down to him by his parents. He understood that this faith concerned a gift that in some way had come from God, but he could not really comprehend or appreciate this gift; most of it remained in its wrapping paper.

As he went through boarding school, Bruce met no one who could further unwrap this gift, the gospel. The gift remained for him not something joyful and liberating but rather, as he wrote, something "stifling, lifeless, funless and boring." Christianity for him meant rules, rituals, and restrictions.

Yet he could not totally discard his childhood faith. One day during his reading he came across a discussion of justification by faith alone. This was a part of the gift that he had not unwrapped, that till then had remained hidden from him. He had thought that to enjoy the blessings of the Christian faith he had to follow its rules, to behave in a prescribed manner, to justify himself by his own righteousness. Now he saw that it was not he who had to justify himself; it was Christ who justified him. He no longer had to "earn" God's acceptance. In Bruce's words: "God accepted me as I was now; acceptance wasn't determined by my first being good or trying to be good; failure did not bring rejection."

This revelation did not mean that Bruce stopped failing. But he saw that he no longer had to strive to avoid failure as he had done in the past; he no longer had to strive to become acceptable to God.

Bruce entered medical school and found himself alternately caught up in hard studying and hard partying. His faith was placed on the back burner. He writes of that period: "My occasional forays to church or the University Christian Union only confirmed my view that evangelical Christianity was a superficial cocktail party without the amelioration of some booze."

After graduation from medical school Bruce served for four years as Naval Medical Officer in the Royal Marine Commandos, not a bad preparation for missionary medicine, when you think of it. During that period he read a book called *After Everest*, by H. Somervell, a medical doctor on one of the early, unsuccessful pre-World War II expeditions to Mount Everest. Subsequently the author had become a medical missionary in India, and in his book he described his life in India as one full of challenge and adventure and robust faith. Such a life was quite in contrast to the "cocktail Christianity" that Bruce had been exposed to.

During that same period Bruce also read a book by another medical doctor, Dr. Martin Lloyd-Jones' *Spiritual Depression—Causes and Cures*. From this book Bruce received a further insight: namely, that though he did not have to strive to be accepted by God, he did need to acquiesce to what God was doing in his life. He learned that if spiritual growth, sanctification, was to progress in his life, he needed to walk with God day by day, to discipline himself, to obey. God wasn't going to do all the work. Yes, God did all the work for salvation; but the work of sanctification He shares with us. For Bruce, this new revelation tore away yet more of the wrapping paper in which his childhood gift of faith had been concealed.

Following his term of service in the Royal Marine Commandos, Bruce set out on a mountaineering expedition to Nepal. He was thirty-four years old, "single, footloose and fancy-free," as he describes himself. His parents were both dead, and his younger siblings were independent. He had visions of becoming a semiprofessional mountaineer. But something was to happen on that expedition to Nepal that would change the direction of his life forever.

What happened is best described in Bruce's own words, taken from a book he contributed to called *God's Doctors Abroad*:

I arrived in Nepal on a mountaineering expedition in 1977. However, a sick colleague kept me at the local 'clinic-cum-hospital' where I became the local doctor in the absence of the Nepalese one. The transition from being a carefree mountaineering medic for a few fit young men to being responsible for the health, however temporarily, of the local population was not something I would have chosen. Being responsible for anything makes demands and imposes restrictions, however small, on a devil-may-care existence. The unwelcome responsibility was compounded by impotence in making diagnoses and giving treatment, there being few facilities and fewer drugs. I was also unfamiliar with anything but Western medicine. The drugs I had brought with me had to be strictly rationed, or we would soon have had none; the ladies dying from tuberculosis in the ward got nothing: there was nothing to give.

A young mother, brought in just before we left, had had a trivial injury the week before, had been carried for three days to a clinic, one day to a further clinic and finally two days to me. During this horrendous journey back and forth over the mountains the abdominal wound had developed gas gangrene, she had aborted and now had peritonitis. I watched her die.

Tragic death was hardly unfamiliar to me after nearly ten years in the business, so the sorrow and anger bursting out were not a usual response; this response was directed at myself; this woman's death, or at least others like it, could be laid fairly at my doorstep. As I frittered away my time, money and expertise on self-indulgent trivia, young mothers were suffering from want of a few pennyworth of care. It was a chastened but happy person who walked out of Nepal, because now I had a personal knowledge of the meaning of ". . . unless a kernel of wheat falls to the ground and dies, it remains only a single seed." Christianity requires 100% of all that we are and have if we are to know its full joy and peace.

For Bruce, the last bit of wrapping paper had finally been removed, and the gift of God's grace and love was now completely revealed to him. Bruce realized that he had been trying to serve two masters, God and money, but as Jesus had said, we can only serve one master. For Bruce, money had become the master. He writes: "The love of money or the love of the things money could buy was indeed the root of all evil for me. I think Jesus was being more literal than we care to think when He said, 'If you have two coats, give one away.'"

From that time Bruce turned from self-centered materialism, and dedicated his life to serving God and his neighbor. He felt that God was calling him to long-term service as a medical missionary in Nepal. And so Bruce applied to join Bible and Medical Missionary Fellowship (BMMF), now called Interserve, an interdenominational mission which sends more workers to Nepal than any other mission agency in the world. It happens to be the mission that my wife Cynthia and I belong to. I can say without hesitation that Bruce was joining a great outfit!

In common with most other mission agencies, BMMF required new candidates to take a year of Bible school, either physically on a campus or by correspondence. Bruce did not look forward to this enforced year of preparation; he viewed a missionary training college as a place of "suffocating piety." However, he discovered All Nations Christian College, north of London, to be anything but suffocating. He found it intellectually stretching, earthily practical, and above all, convivial. So convivial, in fact, that he met two young single women there to whom he took a fancy and who were both planning to become missionaries somewhere in Asia. I am told on reliable authority that it was some time before Bruce could make up his mind which of these two women he should pursue first, Hilda or Heather. He decided on Hilda, and that led shortly to a proposal of marriage, a ready acceptance, and in due course, a wedding. Heather, for her part, went off alone to serve in one of the most isolated and difficult mission stations in Nepal.

Bruce's new bride Hilda had been a Christian since childhood and had had a longstanding desire to become a missionary. However, because of the poor health of her mother, she had been obliged to stay at home. When her mother finally died after six years of illness, Hilda felt free to pursue her missionary calling. She arrived at All Nations the same time Bruce did; and just two days before he proposed, she made up her mind to join Overseas Missionary Fellowship, a mission agency which works in southeast Asia. With Bruce's proposal in hand, however, she switched missions and joined BMMF instead!

After All Nations, Bruce took a six-month refresher course in obstetrics at a hospital in Britain. The one single area of medicine that makes missionary doctors quake is obstetrics. In the Third World, facilities are poor, and the risks to mother and child are high. Many of the mothers will have four, six, or eight other young children at home. There is no leisure time in obstetrics when the doctor can ponder, look up things in his textbooks, or call for help. Two lives are simultaneously at stake, and either or both can be snuffed out in an instant. In my own experience as a missionary doctor, I can say that obstetric cases caused me to tremble more than any other type of case. Bruce's extra six months of training would come in handy.

During Bruce's obstetric training, he and Hilda heard someone talk about a new mission field in a remote area of the Himalayas. The only openings into this new field were for health workers. The people of the area were extremely poor. They were mainly Tibetan Buddhists, among the most unreached in the world. It was a strategic and challenging opportunity, and the Macauleys felt that that was where God wanted them to go. BMMF eventually agreed, and in 1980 Bruce and Hilda took up their work in that rugged and little-known principality in the eastern Himalayas, which would be their home for the next eight years.

Jesus never promised His followers an easy life, and the Macauleys did not find life easy where they lived. The medical work was taxing; the responsibility for the health of so many people was a heavy burden. Bruce was constantly called upon to treat cases he had never seen before, and for which he had no adequate equipment. As time went on, he found himself relying more and more on God for help in making decisions and getting through each day's workload.

Bruce and Hilda also faced health problems of their own. Hilda became ill late in her second pregnancy, which ended in premature labor and the loss of her child. A third pregnancy miscarried as a result of tropical fever. Bruce himself had a severe infection that resulted in a partial paralysis of one of his hands. None of these illnesses would likely have afflicted them had they remained comfortably in Britain. Bruce and Hilda knew what Jesus meant when He warned His disciples to count the cost.

But though the path they trod was not an easy one, still Bruce and Hilda's lives were filled with joy, adventure, and challenge. Their young daughter had a giant playground to grow up in, free from fear of crime and violence and other disadvantages of modern society. The family made lasting friendships, they watched a church grow, they were at peace with God and with themselves. Jesus said that whatever we give up for Him we shall receive a "hundredfold" in return. Bruce and Hilda received a hundredfold.

In the spring of 1987 Hilda again became pregnant. The family looked forward to having a second child; their first, Susan, had long wanted a baby brother or sister. All progressed smoothly until about six weeks before Hilda's due date, when she had an episode of hemorrhage caused by placenta previa, a condition in which the placenta partially blocks the birth canal. If the blockage is very slight, the baby can be delivered from below with minimal risk of serious bleeding; if the blockage is more pronounced, fatal hemorrhage can result, and in such cases delivery by Cesarean section is mandatory.

Bruce was fortunate to have a capable and experienced medical colleague, Brenda Adams, working with him at the hospital. Brenda took primary responsibility for the management of Hilda's pregnancy. She determined that the placenta previa was only marginal, and that Hilda could safely be delivered from below. Bruce's own sister, a missionary obstetrician working in Pakistan, went along with the plan, though she privately wished that her sister-in-law did not have to be delivered in such a remote and minimally equipped hospital.

Hilda had no further bleeding episodes, and so on December 15, Brenda decided that labor should be induced, and that if any bleeding occurred they would immediately resort to a Cesarean section. This is the usual procedure in such situations, and is called a "double setup"— the team is prepared for delivery either from above or from below. Early on the morning of the fifteenth, therefore, Hilda walked up to the hospital from her home, telling neighbors she met along the way, "I'll see you again tomorrow."

Following induction of labor, Hilda began to hemorrhage. At once the team began the Cesarean section, with Brenda operating and Bruce himself taking charge of the anesthesia. A healthy baby girl weighing six pounds was safely delivered, and a sigh of relief went up from the members of the surgical team.

Then, however, something began to go terribly wrong. The placenta could not easily be separated from the inner wall of the uterus, a dangerous condition known as placenta accretia. In such cases the uterus cannot contract normally, and hemorrhage from the uterus continues unabated. Attempts to forcefully separate the placenta led only to further hemorrhage; the only treatment is an immediate removal of the entire uterus, placenta and all.

Already Hilda had lost much blood; her blood pressure was falling rapidly. Other volunteers arrived to donate their blood. Bruce turned over the anesthesia to a nurse anesthetist and hastily scrubbed his hands, put on gown and gloves, and took his place at the operating table to assist Brenda. A postpartum hysterectomy, even under the best conditions, is a very difficult and dangerous procedure. The uterus at delivery is tremendously enlarged and vascular; blood oozes forth from every cut surface.

Bruce and Brenda worked swiftly. The minutes passed by. The nurse anesthetist announced that she could no longer get a blood pressure; others poured in the intravenous solution, and also blood as it became available. The uterus was almost out. The surgeons noticed that the oozing from the cut surfaces was getting less. Then someone shouted, "Look at that!" An assistant lifted a corner of the drape covering the patient, and there on the floor beneath the operating table lay pools of Hilda's blood. She had been bleeding from below all that time; there had been no way to stop it.

There was still no blood pressure. The uterus was removed; the bleeding had stopped. Then for the first time Bruce realized the unthinkable; for the past five minutes he had been operating on a corpse. Hilda was dead.

It was only then that Bruce and Brenda fully realized what had happened. In addition to placenta previa and placenta accretia, Hilda had had yet a third complication of her pregnancy, a very rare complication, often fatal even in the best hospitals of the West: disseminated intravascular coagulation, a condition in which the blood fails to clot normally. This was the real cause of Hilda's death; were it not for that, she would have survived.

Devastated though she was, Brenda led the funeral service at the mission hospital two days later. The outpouring of love and sympathy from hospital staff, local government officials, and neighbors was overwhelming. The coffin was covered with beautiful handmade wreaths, ceremonial silk scarves, and mountains of flowers. Brenda spoke of God's love, and of our hope of eternal life through the resurrected and glorified Savior, Jesus Christ.

The following day Bruce took Hilda's body in the hospital's Land Rover to the capital city of the country, a two-day journey over hairpin turns and precipitous ascents and descents. Four miles outside the capital, a large delegation of expatriate workers and government officials, including the Director General of Health Services for the whole country, had gathered to meet them. The Director General had arranged what amounted to a state funeral, with a slow cortege that wound through the narrow streets of the city that night and again the next morning. The procession ended at midday on the grounds of the central government hospital, where another Christian service was conducted, this time led by one of the missionary doctors serving in that hospital. Again many government officials and hospital staff members heard about the resurrected Christ and about the Christian's hope. Then Hilda was buried next to her infant son, Martin, whom she had lost three years earlier because of premature labor. It could not have escaped the nationals present what it had cost Bruce and Hilda to come to their country to serve their people. And Bruce knows that Hilda's death was not in vain. The words of Jesus that had meant so much to him years earlier now took on their deepest and at the same time most painful meaning: ". . . unless a kernel of wheat falls to the ground and dies, it remains only a single seed. But if it dies, it produces many seeds" (John 12:24).

Inevitably there were some in the Christian community both at home and abroad who questioned Bruce's decision to have Hilda deliver at their out-of-the-way mission hospital. "She should have been brought to the capital; she should have been flown home." Such things are easy to say in retrospect. But Bruce himself gives the best answer in a letter home: "Hilda and I threw in our lot with the people of this country . . . knowing the risks. Of course, we take reasonable precautions to protect ourselves and the children, but in the land of our choosing, maternal and child mortalities are high. Why should we be spared when the people here are not?"

Bruce and Hilda's story does not end here. God specializes in overcoming tragedy and filling empty places. The story goes on, but with a new leading lady. Remember Heather, Bruce's other special friend at All Nations Christian College? She had gone to Nepal as a missionary nurse in 1980, and at the time of Hilda's death eight years later she was still serving there. Heather had spent her first term working in a remote mission station, and in her second term she had moved to an even remoter one, Jumla, in the far northwestern part of the country. I rather imagine it was good preparation for her third mission assignment—becoming the wife of Bruce Macauley.

Heather's own experience in Nepal had been rich and varied. During her time in Jumla she had developed a deep love for the Tibetan Buddhist people, the dominant ethnic and religious group in that area of Nepal. Accessible only by small plane (or a ten-day walk), Jumla and its people had been little touched by the modernization sweeping the rest of Nepal.

One day Heather was called to the home of a woman with a retained placenta. The woman had just delivered, but the placenta had not followed. Heather noticed that there was virtually nothing in the house: no mat for sleeping, just the mud floor; no pots for cooking, not even an earthen stove. All Heather could see in the house were some bloodstained rags. These people didn't even have the basic necessities of life.

After Heather had removed the placenta, the woman was embarrassed and apologetic that she could not offer Heather some tea, since she had nothing in the house. But she did invite Heather to come back after dark—to watch a video, free of charge! Then she showed Heather an adjacent room outfitted with mats, a battery-run video projector, and a white sheet hanging at one end—Jumla's first "movie theater." That was how she made her living. The woman and her family ate at a tea shop across the street, which explained why there were no cooking implements to be found in the house. These people were nothing if not resourceful; they had to be, considering the harshness of the environment in which they lived.

Heather married Bruce in the summer of 1988. Little eight-month-old Jane and six-year-old Susan had a mother again. The family then returned to Bruce's former place of service, where they continued to work until 1990, at which time the government refused further permission for BMMF missionaries to work in the country. After spending some time unsuccessfully seeking permission to work in Tibet, Bruce and Heather decided to return to Nepal instead. There they are presently serving at the Amp Pipal Hospital, the place where Cynthia and I had started our own missionary careers years earlier.

Bruce and Heather still have their sights set on Tibet, yet they have put their heart and soul into their present work, leaving the future in God's hands. They exemplify, as much as any modern missionaries I know, the indomitable spirit of the pioneers of past generations. Bruce has paid the ultimate human price of missionary service: the earthly loss of two loved ones. That is a price still being paid by those called by God to serve in the more difficult areas of the world—among which there is none more difficult than the world of Tibetan Buddhism.

INTO THE NORTHERN REACHES OF THE
TIBETAN BUDDHIST WORLD

CHAPTER NINE

The heart and center of the Tibetan Buddhist world is Tibet itself. Lamaistic Buddhism became well-established there in the sixth and seventh centuries A.D. From there, as we have seen, the influence of Tibetan Buddhism has fanned out, south across the Himalayas to Nepal and Bhutan, west into northern India and Pakistan, and east into the heartland of China. But it is to the northward extension of Tibetan Buddhism that we now turn, in particular to Mongolia and Siberia. While the people of these northern lands would not use the word "Tibetan" to describe their culture, nonetheless their religious practices today can be traced directly back to the influence of Tibetan monks in the court of the Mongol emperor Kublai Khan in the thirteenth century. With minor variations, their religion is essentially the same as that found in Tibet itself.

Kublai Khan was the grandson of Ghengis Khan, the first Mongol emperor. In 1260 A.D., Kublai Khan assumed control of the vast Mongol Empire, which at that time extended from northern China clear across Asia to eastern Europe. The Mongols were a superstitious people, and they sought the aid of the Buddhist lamas of Tibet, who were reputed to have mastery of the occult. Tibetan lamas were invited to the court of Kublai Khan, where they gained favor and exerted increasing influence.

Buddhism, however, was not the only religion Kublai Khan had been exposed to. As early as the seventh century A.D., Nestorian Christians had arrived from Persia, and had introduced Christianity throughout Mongolia and northern China. Kublai Khan himself was interested in this new religion, and is said to have been undecided whether to adopt Christianity or Buddhism as the state religion of his empire. The uncles of the famous Marco Polo happened to be in his court at the time, and in 1266 Kublai Khan sent Marco Polo's uncles back to Europe with the request to Pope Clement IV for:

> an hundred persons of our Christian faith . . . able clearly to prove by force of argument to idolators and other kinds of folk that the Law of Christ was best, and that all other religions were false and naught; and that if they would prove this, [the Khan] and all under him would become Christians and the Church's liegemen.

When Kublai Khan sent this request to the Pope he was the most powerful ruler on earth. This was a missionary opportunity unparalleled in the history of the church. But when Marco Polo's two uncles finally reached Italy three years later, Pope Clement IV had died and no successor had been chosen. Only after another three years was a new Pope selected, and when he looked for men willing to travel to Asia he could find only two. These two set out with the Polo family on the journey Marco Polo made famous, but they soon became terrified by the perils of the trip and turned back. Kublai Khan never got his Christian missionaries. And within a few decades, Tibetan Buddhism had become established as the major religion of the Mongol Empire.

The Mongol Empire lasted only a century and a half, from roughly 1200 A.D. to the mid-1300s. Indeed, it was never really an empire in the traditional sense; it had no permanent capital or center. A visit to Mongolia helps one see why: it is a bleak and inhospitable wasteland. Kublai Khan moved his own court to Beijing, where the environment was more pleasant and he could enjoy the benefits of Chinese civilization. Naturally, he did not endear himself or his countrymen to the Chinese people; after the Mongols left, the Chinese went on to spend the next four centuries building walls to keep any future Mongols out!

I made my own journey to the northern Tibetan Buddhist world in the spring of 1996. I had been asked to serve as a medical consultant on a team exploring possibilities for mission work in the Republic of Buryatia in Siberia. As it worked out, I was able to visit Beijing and Mongolia as well.

I was to meet up with the team leader, my good friend Asbjorn Voreland, in Copenhagen. Asbjorn was director of an "umbrella" organization called Central Asia Fellowship, which had been set up to coordinate and facilitate work among the Tibetan Buddhist peoples of Asia. My KLM flight from the USA was scheduled to arrive in Copenhagen at 4:00 p.m., and then I had to switch to an Air China flight leaving a little before five. The transfer time was too short to allow me to check a suitcase, retrieve it in Copenhagen and then recheck it, and not having my Air China ticket with me (Asbjorn had it in Copenhagen) I couldn't check my luggage straight through. I was thus obliged to cram a month's worth of clothes into one small carry-on and travel, for a change, like most of the world does—light. I needn't have worried. As it turned out, I had a 24-hour layover in Copenhagen: the Air China Boeing 747, on its arrival at the Copenhagen airport, had collided with the jetway and was out of commission. It was interesting watching the airport officials getting a jumbo jet full of passengers onto other flights to Beijing. Asbjorn and I were routed on separate planes to Brussels, where we caught a China Eastern Airlines flight at midnight, which got us to Beijing thirty-six hours later than we had planned. It's best not to schedule trips to Asia too tightly.

Beijing, with its ten million people, is one of the grand cities of the world. The amount of new construction going up is astounding—the very opposite of the former Soviet Union, where partly constructed buildings stand abandoned for lack of funds. From the airport, one drives through miles and miles of modern high-rise apartments, hotels and office buildings. The streets are wide and clean, half the traffic being bicycles and the other half cars. Everything seems to be in order, efficient, regimented. One thinks: "This society functions smoothly; it works." But for all the wonder of this shining, bustling city, one thing struck me more than any other: there seemed little joy in the people's faces. I recall walking an hour down one of the main streets of the city deliberately trying to catch someone's eye; out of thousands I passed only one old man returned my smile. I felt like I had entered a society of robots.

The first day in Beijing we drove forty miles outside the city to see the Great Wall. Yes, it is as impressive in reality as the tourist posters make it out to be. It was a stunning human achievement for its time: four thousand miles of wall wide enough on top for two cars to pass. There are, in addition, hundreds of miles of tributary walls. The walls not only kept the enemy out but provided the emperor with a means of transporting his troops quickly from one trouble spot to another. As an engineering feat, the Great

Wall is a marvel; only the pyramids can compare with it.

But like the pyramids, the Wall was built by the blood and sweat of forced labor. Thousands died over the course of its construction, which took hundreds of years. And the purpose of it all? It was built to protect the emperor and his court and his Imperial Palace, the Forbidden City. It was not built primarily to benefit the Chinese people but rather to benefit their emperor. When we acclaim the Wall, it is the workers we must honor, not their masters.

And who were the enemies the Wall was meant to keep out? Mainly the Mongols, together with their Tibetan Buddhist religion. The Mongols had once sat on the throne in Beijing; the Chinese emperors wanted it never to happen again. The Great Wall was built by one evil kingdom to keep out another.

The road takes you to a pass, a low point in the Wall, where scores of tour buses disgorge their passengers each day. The thoughtful visitor will want to get away from the jostling crowd, from the hawking vendors who physically block your way and are a disgrace to the Chinese Tourism Department. To get away requires walking along the Wall farther than the average tourist is willing to walk, up, up, up as the Wall ascends the rocky, lightly forested mountains that separate Beijing from the flat deserts of Inner Mongolia. And if one chooses to walk at a brisk pace westward along the Wall, one will after half an hour reach a point beyond which the visitor is not permitted to go. The Wall beyond is a ruin, in places utterly broken down. You realize that what you have been walking on is a restoration, almost artificial. And the awe you felt at the massiveness and permanence of this great structure gives way to a sense of its impermanence, even frailty. The pyramids have withstood the test of time much better.

And so the image of the Great Wall that sticks most in my mind is that battered, broken line of rocks snaking its way for miles up and down the jagged mountains of northern China, impregnable no longer, a symbol less of man's power than of his impotence.

The day after visiting the Wall, I went to see what the Wall was designed to protect—the Forbidden City. This is an enormous area in the very center of Beijing containing dozens of impressive palaces, many of them exquisitely beautiful. The Forbidden City easily matches the greatest national treasures of any country in the world. I was the first in line that day to get my ticket, and for a precious half hour I was able to roam the grounds out of sight of tour groups. I could now better appreciate why the Chinese were concerned about keeping such a magnificent cultural treasure safe from the Mongol invaders. My reverie ended when a hundred loudspeakers crackled into life with raspy Chinese music. One couldn't escape it; the speakers were everywhere. The music was meant to enhance the experience, no doubt, but its effect was to rudely jerk one out of the fifteenth century and plunk him down again in the twentieth.

Exiting the Forbidden City one passes under a giant picture of Mao, which looks down on Tienanmen Square. The huge square stretches in front of the Forbidden City and is surrounded on its other three sides by the Hall of the People's Congress, Mao's Mausoleum, and a museum. It was sobering to imagine that just a few years ago the square was filled with students demonstrating for democracy. China is a land in ferment; things are not going to stay the same for long.

Part of that ferment is spiritual. Roughly five percent of Chinese are Christians—over 60 million of them. Considering that fifty years ago there were only a couple million Christians, it is clear that something very interesting has been happening in China—in spite of the authorities' efforts to prevent it. The work of reaching the Tibetan Buddhist peoples, over half of whom reside in China, is going to be greatly affected by the forces taking shape in that great nation.

The next day we flew on Mongolian Airlines to Ulan Bator, the capital of Mongolia. The southern part of Mongolia is desert, the Gobi Desert; the central part is Wyoming-like grassland; and the northern part merges into the forests of Siberia. Mongolia is the least populated nation on earth: 2.2 million people in an area three times the size of France. There are more horses than people. It's not hard to see why. It used to be said: "If you don't behave, you'll be sent to Outer Mongolia"—no grimmer fate being imaginable. I first heard the expression from my mother.

Ulan Bator is a picture of the worst aftermath of the industrial revolution. Dickens could not have created a bleaker city. It is strung out for twenty-five miles along a narrow valley; not a tree can be seen on the hills to either side. The city's 600,000 people, almost a quarter of Mongolia's total population, live in shabby apartment blocks interspersed among Communist-era factories. Winter is seven months long with no snow. Old tires, bits of metal, rubbish and broken glass lie everywhere. It is not safe to let young children play on the streets. Not surprisingly, the chief source of cheer for most people is the bottle. The Russia-dependent economy is tottering. Unemployment is rising, living standards are falling; prospects for the future are not encouraging. And as if things weren't bad enough, even as we arrived, over four hundred forest and prairie fires were raging out of control, the worst in Mongolia's history, resulting in the loss of over one-fourth of the country's grasslands and forests.

Yet there is a strange optimism to be detected in the faces of the people, especially the young. Mongolians are free at last from Soviet domination, free to pursue their own national aspirations. In the 1996 elections, the people retired the Communist hierarchy and installed a government committed to democracy. Defying the general pessimism is a sense of expectancy. Like the former Soviet Union, Mongolia is in the throes of momentous change.

As we sat down to supper in the hotel dining room that first evening in Ulan Bator, an extraordinary thing happened which can only be laid to God's divine intervention. For some months I had been hoping to meet with a top official of the United Bible Societies (UBS) concerning some important issues that had arisen in connection with the new translation of the Nepali Bible, on which I had been working for many years. I had hoped to see the appropriate person at the UBS headquarters in England earlier in the year, but was unable to meet him there. The matter had been weighing on my mind ever since.

As Asbjorn and I sat down to supper I noticed a Western man across the dining room sitting at a table by himself. I commented to Asbjorn that he "looked like one of us"—the missionary type, you know—vigorous, intelligent, good-looking. And then I did something I don't often do: I went over to the man and asked him what he was doing in Mongolia.

"I'm with the United Bible Societies," he said. "I have been visiting the Mongolian Bible Society folks here in Ulan Bator."

"What do you do with UBS?" I asked.

"I'm in charge of all translation work in Asia."

This was the very man I needed to see! He said he was leaving the next day, so I asked to have breakfast with him so that I could share with him what was on my mind.

The next morning, as we reached the end of our discussion

about the Nepali translation, he suddenly pulled out his pocket calendar. He said, "My goodness, do you know what? I have a meeting scheduled tomorrow in Hong Kong with the new secretary of the Nepal Bible Society. Tomorrow I will be able to raise this matter with him in person."

I had seen God do this kind of thing before, but never with such geographic extravagance. He had perfectly coordinated the movements of three of His people—American, Australian and Nepali—between USA, Mongolia, Hong Kong, and Nepal. If you had asked me to name the least likely city in the world for a chance meeting to occur, I might well have said, "Ulan Bator." Not any longer.

After supper that first evening in Ulan Bator I went for a stroll along the crumbling sidewalks of the city's one main street. I hadn't been walking two minutes when suddenly, with loud crackling and sparkling, the overhead boom of a passing electric trolley bus became detached from its wire and swung wildly in my direction. Fortunately the springs at its base were strong, and within a minute the driver had climbed the bus and reattached the boom. On came the lights and the bus rumbled off.

Two miles down the street I came to the central square of the city. It was dark by this time. Along one side of the square was the imposing, columned Hall of the People's Congress. In the center of the square stood a large statue of a warrior mounted on a horse—Ghengis Khan, Mongolia's founder and national hero. Large crowds of young people stood milling about in the dark—the heirs of Ghengis. But the chief thing that caught my eye was the opera house facing the square—not the opera house itself so much, but rather what was going on inside, a live rock concert booming out through the walls and windows, with revolving colored lights that swept across the people in the square, momentarily lighting up their faces in yellow, red, and green.

Ghengis Khan ruled before Buddhism reached Mongolia. He was a shamanist, as were most of the peoples of Central Asia. When Buddhism spread north during Kublai Khan's time, it easily absorbed shamanism, as it had done earlier in Tibet. This shamanistic Buddhism was practiced throughout Mongolia until the Communists took power in Russia and imposed atheism on their satellites. Only now, after seventy years, is religion beginning to again play a part in the life of the nation. And one religion that is going to play a part is Christianity.

In 1991 there were no Christian churches in Mongolia and virtually no known Christians—the only exception I know of being the Mongolian wife of a British Bible translator. But with the collapse of Communism, foreign workers have come into Mongolia; by last count almost fifty Christian agencies had set up offices in Ulan Bator. And already there are over two dozen Mongolian congregations in the city—half of them started by Korean missionaries. Some of these churches meet in movie theaters, and ten of them have over four hundred members each, mostly young people. The service we attended was filled with enthusiastic young Mongolians radiating the joy of the Lord. Many are at various stages of faith; in some cases "conversion" seems to be incremental. In the beginning they come for the novelty, the entertainment, the music; in the end they encounter Jesus Christ and their lives are changed forever.

The leader of the particular church we attended was a young Mongolian businessman in his thirties, one of the most winsome Asian Christians I have ever met. He had been led to Christ five years earlier by a Westerner who had come to teach English in Mongolia. Now the young Mongolian is not only the leader of his own church but is also one of three key leaders in all of Ulan Bator coordinating the work of many Christian agencies. That English teacher had no idea when he went out that he would be God's chosen instrument for raising up within five short years one of the most important Christian leaders in all of Mongolia.

I was privileged to meet one of the Korean missionaries in Ulan Bator, Pastor Lee. He was explaining to a public meeting of Christians how his work got started in Ulan Bator. He had come in the early 1990s to establish a Korean-style church, in which he would start as leader and then gradually turn leadership over to the Mongolians after eight to ten years. He assumed it would take that long to train indigenous leaders. But Pastor Lee had a profound experience with the Holy Spirit that changed his ministry. He saw that his attitude and his relationship with the nationals in his church and also with his forty fellow-Korean missionaries was not what it should be. He publicly repented, and determined to turn over the leadership of his church within the year. To his amazement, he discovered that God had already raised up many leaders among the Mongolian members of his church. That church has gone on to become one of the most thriving churches in Mongolia, with seventeen cell groups instead of the one cell group Pastor Lee had led just two years earlier. Pastor Lee told us, "Ever since I stopped doing things 'Korean-style,' the Lord has blessed my ministry and my relationships with other Christians." If I had to pick one outstanding quality of Pastor Lee's life, it would be humility, a rare and precious commodity on the mission field.

As of mid-1999, there are estimated to be ten thousand Mongolian Christians. Ten years ago, there were none. God is doing a great work in this Tibetan Buddhist land. However, for foreign workers, it is one of the most physically and spiritually difficult fields I know of. There are risks at every hand—rising crime, for example. The day before our arrival a Japanese school teacher was strangled with his own necktie by drunken students in the same apartment block where several missionary families live; he had refused to loan the students money. Health risks are high too. Not long before we arrived, the leading surgeon of Ulan Bator had died of salmonella food poisoning from bad mayonnaise—in the same hotel where we were staying. The Christians in Mongolia, both foreign and national, need the prayers and support of the world church. And they need more workers to join them. "Ask the Lord of the harvest, therefore, to send out workers into his harvest field" (Matt. 9:38).

STEPHEN COLLINS AND THE MONGOLIAN
BIBLE SOCIETY

CHAPTER TEN

A s pioneer missionaries extend the frontiers of the church into new nations, a half-step behind them must come the Bible translators. Indeed, for smaller tribal groups, the translators themselves are often the first ones in. No church will stand without the Word of God being made available in either oral or written form. The story of Scripture translation is as engrossing as any aspect of the missionary endeavor. William Carey set the stage for modern translators in the early 1800s; he and his team produced Scriptures in more than a dozen languages.

No doubt inspired by Carey's example, the London Missionary Society in 1817 sent three missionaries with their families on a 4,000-mile sled ride to an area of Siberia just north of the Mongolian border. There, in addition to their other evangelistic activities, they managed to translate the entire Bible into Mongolian. It took almost thirty years, and was not without cost. One of the missionaries, three of the wives, and several of the children died on the field.

The Word of God is a powerful weapon in the hands of the church, and the enemy will go to great lengths to suppress the Word and snuff out those who labor to make the Word available. It is not an accident that translators are often called to pay the ultimate price, the offering of their lives. Not many years ago one of the missionaries of my own home church, while working at his desk in Papua, New Guinea, was axed to death by his own translation assistant. A young nurse midwife, Pam Love, was working in Bhutan, and in her spare time she began translating the New Testament into the Bhutanese language. First her language helper, a believer, died of leukemia, and shortly thereafter she herself died of ovarian cancer. Peter Rapgey, a former Tibetan monk-turned-Christian pastor in Kalimpong, translated almost the entire Old

Testament into modern Tibetan, and in the process lost two sons to resistant tuberculosis before succumbing himself to the same disease in 1995. Tucking oneself away in a quiet study and sitting at a desk all day long does not give one immunity from the spiritual warfare that rages on the mission field and which affects not only mind and spirit but body as well.

Not only are the translators under attack, but their translations get attacked also. William Carey's entire warehouse went up in flames, with the loss of many translations still in progress. After his death, Peter Rapgey's Old Testament was almost destroyed by the monsoon rain and dampness of northern India. Pam Love's Bhutanese New Testament has been totally lost, and so a new translation has been started from scratch. And up in Mongolia, that original Mongolian Bible, published by the London Missionary Society in 1846, fell victim to the Bolshevik Revolution, and no copies have survived the Communist era.

Communist Mongolia. One could not imagine a more barren land both physically and spiritually. No believers; no Scripture. But back in the darkest days of the Cold War, 1972, a young Englishman named Stephen Collins came out to Mongolia under the British Council—the first time he'd ever been abroad—and set in motion a chain of events that would culminate in the Mongolian Bible Society and also Mongolia's very first church, which held its opening service in Ulan Bator on September 23, 1990, with six believers attending.

I first met Stephen Collins in the two-room office of the Mongolian Bible Society on my last afternoon in Ulan Bator. He was covered with engine grease. He looked as if he'd been working on the insides of a truck—which, in fact, was precisely the case. You remember the saying: missionaries need to know how to do everything. He had agreed to meet me and tell me his story, and his story turned out to be one of the most unique and instructive stories I have yet heard.

Stephen grew up in an English Brethren family; he hated church and considered his parents hypocrites. At age nine he had some kind of emotional religious experience that did not involve repentance. He was attracted to God and began to search for Him, but couldn't find Him. As he entered his teens, Stephen became interested in doing Christian work, but he couldn't accept Christianity, especially the kind he found in the average English church. He failed to understand how God could create people who He knew beforehand were going to hell. Furthermore, he felt that Christians had created God in their own image; their very lives seemed to deny the supernatural. He concluded that they had merely "auto-suggested" themselves into some sort of faith.

So, spurred by a desire to confirm these negative impressions, Stephen enrolled in a Bible school. That, he says, convinced him there was no God. "For me, Bible school was one hundred percent proof that God didn't exist." Other students "got up his nose." Every Monday evening he had to endure what was called "testimony night," during which students would get up and describe nonexistent blessings and confess nonexistent sins. Stephen considered it all to be a "pack of drivel."

One Monday morning Stephen decided to speak at the testimony meeting that evening. He planned to say that he had found only one true statement in the entire Bible: ". . . seek, and you will find" (Matt. 7:7). Then he planned to add: "I sought—and I found that God did not exist. Hallelujah! That statement is true."

Stephen was pleased with his plan; he would prove himself the only honest student in the school. He had concluded that all spiritual experience was unreal, just autosuggestion. He was convinced not only that there was no God but that it was pointless even to create a god— man didn't need a god. And finally, Stephen considered the Bible to be "rubbish." It was filled with internal discrepancies. Was there one beggar or two in the story of blind Bartimaeus, for example?

Stephen thought that before he got up to speak at the testimony meeting it would strengthen his case if he could find some more of these discrepancies. He needed more proof that the Bible was rubbish. So he started out that Monday morning reading Matthew's Gospel. He couldn't stand the Revised Standard Version: he thought it was badly written, uninteresting—"like chewing on cardboard." So he read Matthew in the New English Bible instead. He sat down and read it straight through as fast as he could—one and a half hours. And his life has never been the same since.

Two things happened as Stephen read Matthew that day. He realized that he was reading the account of an eyewitness—not a yarn spinner or fable writer—an eyewitness to certain events. Matthew had to have actually seen the events he described in order to write the way he did. This was not the impression Stephen had been expecting to receive—quite the opposite. But that rapid, nonstop reading of Matthew gave Stephen a vision of Jesus he had never had before. It was as if the individual incidents in Jesus' life had coalesced into one compelling reality.

The second thing that happened to Stephen as he read was that he became aware of God's presence. The God who he had been certain did not exist was there beside him. By the time Stephen had finished reading, God's presence was overwhelming. Stephen had never truly prayed before, but now he prayed. He fell on his knees and repented of his sins and asked God to forgive him. And he accepted Jesus as his Savior and Lord.

That night at the testimony meeting, Stephen said not a word.

Stephen's proclivities as a student leaned toward science and engineering rather than to the arts. Language, especially, he considered was for sissies. In his high-school French final exam, he managed a score of three out of a possible hundred.

He looked on missions a little bit like he looked on language. He considered missions the most boring aspect of Christianity. The only things that stood out in his mind about missions were bad slides and dysentery. The few missionaries he met struck him as social misfits. He had read a book once by George Bernard Shaw entitled, *The Missionary*. In it a young English lady, having failed to find a husband, decides to become a missionary and sails to Africa. The Africans aren't interested in her ideas, but she becomes interested in theirs. She ends up marrying a black African and producing a pile of coffee-colored kids. That was what missionaries were like in Stephen's mind. They were pathetic people, naive, easily duped. Stephen was certain of one thing: he'd never become a missionary.

After Bible school Stephen worked for a Christian phone-counseling service for several years. Toward the end of that period he married a Christian girl who worked for the same service. Soon after that, he began to feel that he ought to serve God in London. During this time he continued studying the Scriptures and praying. He was growing in his understanding that commitment to Christ cannot be partial, it must be total. And so he came to a point where one day he said to God, "Whatever you want me to do with my life, I will do it. Just show me."

Very shortly thereafter, Stephen came across Romans 15:20, where Paul writes: "It has always been my ambition to preach the gospel where Christ was not known, so that I would not be building on someone else's foundation." Where was Christ "not known"? It certainly wasn't London.

Several years earlier Stephen had read a *National Geographic* article about Mongolia, which described the country as being firmly atheistic with not even a vestige of Christianity to be found. One of his teachers at the time told him (incorrectly) that the gospel had never reached Mongolia. Stephen tucked this information in a back corner of his mind and promptly forgot about it. But now it suddenly came to the front of his mind. Mongolia was the place God wanted him to serve, the place where Christ was not known. Stephen, the one who had declared he'd never be a missionary, the one who had never even set foot outside of Britain, felt with total certainty that God was calling him to Mongolia. The year was 1968. Sadly, his wife did not seem to share in this calling.

Stephen sent letters of inquiry to forty-two different mission agencies. Some wondered if Mongolia was part of the Soviet Union; others wondered if it was part of China. No one had really thought about Mongolia. Here was a county with no Christians, no Bibles, and no one had plans to do anything about it. Mongolia was off everyone's map. Furthermore, Stephen saw no way to even reach Mongolia; in his mind that proved it was unreached! That was proof of his calling.

But how could he get there? How could he persuade his wife to join him?

One day he happened to be doing some gardening for an elderly lady when he heard an almost audible voice speak to him: "I have set before you an open door and no one can shut it."

A short time later he read of a course in Mongolian studies being offered at Leeds University in northern England. A degree in either the Russian or Chinese language was a prerequisite. Stephen felt God telling him to write to Leeds University and express interest in the course though he did not have the required language degrees, and would they please send him a book or tapes on how to learn Mongolian. He wrote the letter, and promptly he received a reply back saying there was no reason he couldn't enter the course; enclosed was an application form for the fall semester. Stephen filled out the form, sent it back, and was immediately accepted.

Stephen had no money for the tuition, so he talked to his pastor about it. Within one week the entire amount necessary to cover all his expenses had been raised. In 1970 Stephen began his Mongolian studies at Leeds University.

During that first year, the man who had once thought languages were for sissies took a crash course in Mongolian. He recalls being "scared stiff." He said to God, "It will be impossible for me to learn Mongolian if you do not help. You'll have to help me." Stephen knew he had no natural aptitude for language study, nor even an interest in it. But he set his mind to master Mongolian, counting on God's help to do so. He ended up first in the class.

Toward the end of that year, Stephen learned that a cultural exchange program with Mongolia had been set up under the British Council, and that he was eligible to apply to be an exchange student; one place was offered each year. Stephen applied and got the place. That summer, before leaving for Mongolia, he took a translation course run by the Summer Institute of Linguistics. Also during that summer, Stephen's wife left him.

Stephen spoke to me frankly about his marriage. It was no doubt one of the saddest and most difficult chapters in his life. Though both he and his wife were Christians, they simply did not "hit it off." They did not appreciate the work required to make a marriage successful. Stephen feels they were both naive; they thought things would work out automatically. Stephen readily takes the major blame for his wife leaving him; he shows no bitterness. Yet it was surely with a heavy heart that Stephen set out for Mongolia in that fall of 1972, to go through that door that God had so amazingly opened up for him, and which no man could close.

On his arrival in Ulan Bator, Stephen was given a room with two Mongolian students. He spoke nothing but Mongolian, and quickly became fluent. At the university in Ulan Bator, Stephen was expected to give lectures on English literature; therefore, he needed to select an English work which he could translate into Mongolian for use in his classroom. He chose an "English" work written by a fellow named Mark, and proceeded to translate it into Mongolian. And that was the beginning of Stephen's career as a Bible translator. When his year in Mongolia was up, he sewed a copy of his Mongolian translation of Mark into the bottom of his suitcase, and smuggled it out of the country into Siberia, and then via the Trans-Siberian Railroad out of the Soviet Union and back into Europe. When he got back to England, he resumed his studies at Leeds University, this time adding the Russian language to his study program.

Over the next five years, Stephen sought to return to Mongolia, but could not. He continued his studies at Leeds. On the side he began a translation of the New Testament into Mongolian, carrying on from his earlier work on Mark. He kept in touch with the Mongolians studying at Leeds as exchange students. By 1978 he had completed degrees in both Mongolian and Russian, and had finished one half of his translation of the New Testament. His next step was to earn a doctorate in Mongolian studies.

Meanwhile his marriage remained essentially dead. His wife refused to rejoin him and also refused to divorce him. No reconciliation seemed possible. Though Stephen's studies were going well, he was lonely and unhappy. He was not at peace, either emotionally or spiritually.

Then in 1978 a second chance came to go to Mongolia under a British Council scholarship. This time Stephen's primary purpose for going was to do research for his doctorate. He also planned to complete the Mongolian New Testament. After arriving in Ulan Bator he reestablished his connection with the university and began his studies. Then he met Ulaa.

Ulaa was an attractive Mongolian graduate student. She and Stephen hit it off immediately and soon were deeply in love. They were drawn into greater and greater intimacy, and eventually into adultery. Stephen figured that his life and service as a Christian had come to an end.

Stephen was tormented both by his illicit love and also by guilt. He thought, "God has rejected me forever; He will not forgive such a grievous sin." At the same time, he had put Ulaa herself into great jeopardy. She was already under suspicion because of her relationship with a Westerner; the Mongolian authorities were watching her every move. If Stephen deserted her, she would likely end up in prison for being the girlfriend of a "spy."

In 1979 Stephen reached the lowest point in his life. Unable any longer to endure alienation from God, Stephen cried out to Him for mercy. He confessed his sin and asked for forgiveness. But he had no assurance that he'd been forgiven; he still felt he was under God's condemnation.

Then Stephen realized that the basis of forgiveness is Jesus Christ alone, that forgiveness is not for a sin but for the sinner. The punishment for the sin had been carried out on Calvary; because of Christ, Stephen was no longer condemned. And Stephen saw in a way he'd never seen before what Christ's death on the cross had wrought for him. And he freely repented, and began to experience the forgiveness Christ had promised.

For some months Stephen felt a new power and freedom to witness. He began leading Mongolians to Christ. Ulaa herself became a Christian and began to witness fearlessly. But then suddenly, in early 1980, Stephen was arrested for evangelistic activities and expelled from the country. Ulaa, too, was arrested, and the last thing Stephen knew before he left Mongolia was that Ulaa had been sentenced as a spy and was facing an eight-year jail sentence. Stephen returned to England and did not see Ulaa again for seven years.

Ulaa, in Stephen's words, "went through hell." The Mongolian authorities ordered her to give up her Christianity. They said she only believed in Christ because of her love for Stephen. She spent the next seven years in and out of prison, but never once did she deny her faith.

Meanwhile back in England, Stephen's wife finally divorced him in order to marry someone else. Stephen himself set about to finish the Mongolian New Testament. When it was completed, a Youth With A Mission (YWAM) team carried copies of it into Mongolia, and Ulaa helped distribute them. Great interest was stimulated among the Mongolians, and the YWAM team got their pictures on the front page of Ulan Bator's main newspaper. This further increased interest in the New Testament. Finally the authorities clamped down and arrested the YWAM team and Ulaa along with them.

This created an even greater stir. So the government expelled the team from the country and let Ulaa out of prison in hopes that the commotion would die down. The world Christian community was quick to criticize the rashness and inexperience of the YWAM team, but in the short time they were in Mongolia, they had managed to circulate dozens of copies of the New Testament and create a widespread desire among the populace to learn more about this new religion. God has a way of using the rash and inexperienced to get things done that the cautious and experienced might never do.

In the late 1980s, the case of Stephen and Ulaa reached the attention of the British government. As the economy of the Soviet Union began to decline in its waning years, Mongolia turned more and more to the West for economic aid.

According to Stephen, Britain agreed to assist Mongolia, but only on the condition that the Mongolian government permit Stephen and Ulaa to marry. Queen Elizabeth herself sent a letter to the Mongolian ambassador in London on their behalf. Two months later permission was granted, and Stephen, a Mongolian visa in hand, was on his way to Ulan Bator to be reunited with Ulaa after a wait of seven and a half years.

One of Stephen and Ulaa's major responsibilities during the past six or so years in Ulan Bator has been the establishment of the Mongolian Bible Society, which is affiliated with the United Bible Societies. In addition to their work in Mongolian, they are sponsoring a translation of the New Testament into the language of the Buryat people, a separate Tibetan Buddhist group of half a million, who live in the northern part of Mongolia and in the Russian Republic of Buryatia. The translator, Baldorgin Tserendash, himself a Buryat, is presently midway through the New Testament.

Tserendash was introduced to Christ by Stephen Collins on Stephen's second trip to Mongolia in 1978. Before that, Tserendash had worked for eighteen years as an official censor for Mongolia's communist government. Tserendash's wife had scrofula (glandular tuberculosis), and he attributes her healing to Stephen's prayers at that time. During Stephen's long wait in Britain during the 1980s, Tserendash continued reading his Russian Bible and growing in faith. When Stephen finally returned to Mongolia, Tserendash began going to the church in Ulan Bator that Stephen started. Now they are partners in the work of preparing Scripture and distributing it throughout the northern reaches of the Tibetan Buddhist world. This is the fruit of the labors of a man who—with the exception of his failed first marriage—has been otherwise faithful to the calling God has given him. May we also be found faithful.

We move now to Tserendash's people, the Buryats, and our journey will take us northward on the Trans-Siberian Railroad into the heart of Siberia.

THE REPUBLIC OF BURYATIA

CHAPTER ELEVEN

The Republic of Buryatia lies due north of Mongolia and to the east of Lake Baikal. It is the size of France and has 1.2 million inhabitants, two-thirds of whom are ethnic Russians, with the remaining third being Buryats. Another 100,000 Buryats live in adjacent republics of Russia, and 40,000 live in northern Mongolia. Up until now there has been almost no mission work specifically targeting these Buryat people; they constitute one of the last true frontiers in missions.

Only a handful of foreign Christian workers are currently serving in Buryatia, and those are all recent arrivals. The Russian Orthodox church has been making some gains since the fall of communism, but it is not a vital evangelistic presence. A few Russian Protestant groups exist, but again they minister mainly to ethnic Russians. There is no purely Buryat church.

Most Buryats speak Russian fluently, but in the rural areas, especially, they still prefer to use their mother tongue. The Buryats have for centuries been Lamaistic (Tibetan) Buddhists, and now with the restraints of Soviet state atheism removed, they are more openly following their traditional beliefs. It is possible for Russian Christians to serve as witnesses to the Buryat people and some are doing so. But there is also at the present time a unique opportunity for foreign Christians to aid the Buryats both materially and spiritually. Buryatia is in need of technological assistance, especially in the health field, and the government has turned to the West and to the technologically advanced countries of Asia to provide such assistance. Indeed, the primary purpose of our visit to Buryatia was to ascertain the precise areas of need and then to set up a partnership of mission groups that could channel assistance to the region in a coordinated manner.

Assistance they certainly need. As in the rest of the former Soviet Union and in Mongolia, the economy is in chaos. There is 40 percent unemployment in the cities, and up to 60 percent unemployment in the villages. Many people have no hope; they have become fatalistic, and believe that nothing they do will make any difference. Even among the few Christians this pessimistic outlook can be found. Now is the greatest opportunity in nearly a century for the worldwide Christian community to reach out to these people and give them true hope.

The Trans-Siberian Railroad takes twenty-four hours to transport its passengers from Ulan Bator to Ulan Ude, the capital of Buryatia. The distance is only three hundred miles, but much time is taken up at the Russian border while custom officials inspect the train, search for smuggled goods and people, and actually count the money in the passengers' wallets. The first part of the ride through northern Mongolia takes one out of the rolling grasslands into forest-covered mountains; then, crossing the border, the route follows a broad, winding river valley surrounded on either side by the vast forestland of Siberia.

We had been joined on the trip to Siberia by a third team member, Ernie Addicott, who represented an organization called Interdev, which specializes in bringing mission agencies together to form partnerships. Ernie had been a pilot with Mission Aviation Fellowship in Africa, and proved to be a most genial traveling companion, full of insight, wit and good humor. He sported a large handlebar mustache, which he hoped one day would grow wide enough to be seen from behind. He could have passed for a Cossack.

We arrived in Ulan Ude, population 400,000, at 10:30 p.m., feeling very much in need of a hot shower after the gritty train journey. We had no hotel reservations and no rubles, but Asbjorn knew of a hotel on the city's main square that would surely provide hot running water. No one spoke English, including the taxi driver. When he dropped us off at the Hotel Baikal, he was chagrined to find that we had only dollars with which to pay him. The elderly matron behind the reception counter at the hotel also spoke no English and also did not want dollars. It now being after 11:00 p.m., there was no hope of exchanging money, and the hotel people gave the impression that they couldn't care less whether we slept in their hotel or out on the street. Ulan Ude is not yet set up to receive tourists—certainly not those coming by rail from Mongolia.

Finally the lady behind the counter relented and accepted our dollars as a deposit for one night's stay. We were led up to our three single rooms, and quickly discovered that there was no hot water. In Russia, hot water is provided centrally by the city, and that week the city's hot-water pipes were being repaired and so the hot water had been shut off everywhere. J. Paul Getty himself couldn't have found a hotel room in Ulan Ude with hot water that night.

As it turned out, my room didn't have any water at all, hot or cold. It took me fifteen minutes to persuade a grumpy floor matron to at least come and see what I was gesticulating about. I was finally given another room, for which I was doubly thankful since the first room had had no toilet seat either. And this was the second-best hotel in Buryatia! That night I took the coldest shower of my life; it was a wonder the water flowed at all. There was no mistaking I was in Siberia.

The next morning Asbjorn tried to phone our contact person in Ulan Ude, whom he had met on a previous visit, but was only able to leave a questionably understood message with a third party. We changed some money into rubles at a bank and then returned to the hotel to pay for our next night's stay. The same lady behind the reception counter took the rubles and then handed back the dollars we had given her the previous evening. But when we tried to give her more rubles to reserve our rooms for the second night, she wouldn't take the money. Perhaps she couldn't understand what we wanted; it's hard to have a conversation when the only words you know are "nyet" and "da."

Then we noticed some rolls of toilet paper for sale on a table behind the reception counter. Since our rooms had not been provided with that commodity, we deemed it prudent to buy three rolls right then and there. After all, a busload of tourists might suddenly arrive and snap it all up, and we would be left without. So with some difficulty we managed to purchase three rolls and I was elected to take them up to my room for safekeeping. My two colleagues were to wait for me out on the front steps of the hotel, and then we planned to stroll around the city. In the evening, Asbjorn would again try to get in touch with his contact person.

Not wanting to keep my friends waiting long, I ran up the stairs to my room, but then remembered I didn't have my room key. I had left it with the floor matron, which was the required procedure. There was a large box attached to the top of her desk with a slot in it, where you deposited your key each time you left the floor. The matron was not there. However, an ancient, medalled veteran of the Great Patriotic War was sitting in her seat, perhaps filling in for her while she was taking a break. The old veteran was partly blind and partly deaf, very arthritic, and missing a leg, but full of good cheer nonetheless. After some time I made him understand I needed my key, so he tried to open the door of the key box to get my key out. It wouldn't open; it was evidently locked. So a long search for the key to the key-box door ensued. The desk had many drawers, all of them filled with all sorts of stuff, including many keys to other drawers and boxes, each of which had to be tried of course; so in the end it took almost ten minutes to locate the correct key. But then, try as he might, the jolly old veteran couldn't make the key work, a circumstance that clearly caused him more merriment than distress. The key went into its slot and turned all right, but the door still would not open. I thought of my friends waiting impatiently for me outside the hotel; getting the toilet paper had been mainly my idea in the first place, and now nearly fifteen minutes had passed.

Suddenly the old veteran erupted in laughter. He had found the cause of the problem. The door to the key box hadn't been locked at all; it was being blocked from opening by a thick piece of glass on the desk top that served as a writing surface. When the old man finally got hold of himself, he slid the glass half an inch to the left, and presto, the door swung open and there lay my key. I hastily put the toilet paper in my room, returned the key to the still chuckling veteran, and ran down the stairs, fully expecting to find my friends in the terminal stages of exasperation. The whole caper had taken seventeen minutes.

True, for the first ten minutes or so they had indeed been getting exasperated. But just then, two missionary couples had showed up at the hotel looking for us. They had heard indirectly that some foreigners had arrived at the hotel the night before, and they suspected it might be us. If it hadn't been for the toilet paper, we would have missed those two couples—and they were to prove crucial for the success of our visit. To begin with, they knew of an empty, fully furnished apartment we could stay in for free. We then knew that it had been God who had prevented us from paying for that second night's room at the hotel.

In addition to successfully meeting our objectives in Siberia, getting to know these two couples was just as much a highlight of the trip. They represent the new generation of Christian workers—bright, energetic, well-informed, and filled with optimism. If these couples are any measure, the missionary movement will be in good hands as their generation takes leadership. The first couple, the Willoughbys, are Americans from Baton Rouge, Louisiana. I was surprised to learn that the one church in Louisiana where I have been a missions speaker was the very church they were married in. They have five boys, ages roughly four to eleven. And they all live together in a happy, rollicking three-room flat on the sixth floor of one of those faceless, drab apartment buildings that you see scattered everywhere in the cities of Russia.

Asbjorn told us he never trusted the elevators in Russian apartment buildings; he said he'd rather use the stairway. Ernie, somewhat on the hefty side and no lover of stairs, thought that Asbjorn's concern was unwarranted, and I agreed. It turned out that on our second visit to the Willoughbys, Asbjorn wasn't with us, so Ernie and I, of course, took the elevator. Between the fifth and sixth floors the lights abruptly went out and the elevator jerked to a stop. And there we were, in the pitch darkness. After a minute, we began to think we might be stuck there for some time. I remembered a story I'd heard somewhere about a man getting stuck on a Soviet elevator—and how long had he waited? Hours, I seemed to recall. After a brief prayer, Ernie and I decided a little shouting for help wouldn't hurt, so we did that for a few minutes. It was soon evident, however, that we were in a remarkably soundproof box; our shouts were going nowhere. Then, after five or six minutes, the lights flickered on and the car lurched upward, and we were soon at our floor and out the door. I rather think Ernie and I have now swung over to Asbjorn's position—though it wouldn't do to admit it openly.

John and Carla Willoughby had met as students at Louisiana State University in 1985. Two years before that, Campus Crusade for Christ had held their Christmas convention in Kansas City, KC-83, and Carla had attended along with twenty thousand others. She heard Billy Graham, the keynote speaker, tell the audience: "Don't stand up to signal a commitment to Christ unless you really mean it. Be ready to go anywhere and do anything and say anything that the Lord asks you. It won't be easy; it will mean sweat and tears."

Carla took Graham's message to heart. She promised the Lord that she would go anywhere He asked. Over the next year she heard about the need in Russia and felt God calling her to go there. In the summer of 1985, she went to western Russia on a short-term Campus Crusade for Christ-sponsored project, and saw God not only provide for her needs but also enable her to witness effectively. As a result of that summer's experience, Carla felt even more clearly that she was being called to long-term service in Russia.

Then that fall Carla met John, who had also felt called to missions, but in Mongolia. John was strongly attracted to Carla, but she was dating a fellow named Alex at the time, and so John concluded that she was not the girl God had selected for him. But he couldn't get Carla out of his mind. Finally John told the Lord, "I will totally give that girl up, and concentrate only on your will and the work you have appointed me to do."

Unbeknownst to John, Carla that very week had decided she should break up with Alex. She told God, "I don't want to date anymore. Just bring me the man you have chosen for me."

Carla felt the Lord say to her: "John Willoughby is going to be your husband." He had given her up, but the Lord had given him to her.

That same day, Carla found herself sitting next to John in a meeting at their church in Baton Rouge. She said to him, "Alex and I are no longer dating."

"What?" said John, jumping from his seat. Then he told Carla of his love for her. She was amazed. Eleven days later he proposed.

John and Carla were married in the summer of 1986. John spent the next three years in the army, and ended up in Kuwait during the Gulf War, leaving Carla at home with three babies in diapers. After the army, John enrolled in a masters program at New Orleans Baptist Theological Seminary, cramming three years of study into two. His main focus was the formation of cell-group churches as a primary ministry.

During seminary John continued to feel called to Mongolia; Carla, for her part, was still thinking of western Russia. One day a professor of Carla's received a letter outlining the need for someone to start up work in the Republic of Buryatia in Siberia, and the professor showed the letter to John. John was intrigued, so he took the letter home and showed it to Carla. If someone had mentioned Siberia to her before that day, she says she would have shuddered and recoiled from the prospect of going there. But she found that the Lord had given her a strange peace about Siberia. She asked the Lord for confirmation that she and John were to go to Siberia. The next Sunday she couldn't attend her regular church service, so she listened to a radio broadcast instead; and to her surprise, the preacher on the radio spoke of the spiritual needs in Siberia. Carla felt this to be the confirmation she had asked for.

Carla asked the Lord, "Why do I have such peace about taking my family to Siberia?" By this time she had four boys, and had adopted a fifth.

The Lord said to her, "Did you not tell me at KC-83 that you would go anywhere and do anything for me? That is why you have peace. Those who submit their wills to me always experience peace. You have seen me provide for all your needs up till now. You can be at peace for the future too."

After that, neither John nor Carla had any doubt about their call to Buryatia. They had no idea what living conditions in Siberia would be like, what the work would be like. But today they are in their second year of fruitful ministry in Ulan Ude, raising five happy boys in the process.

John's main job is teaching English, but on the side he and Carla keep an open home, and many young people come to visit. Asbjorn, Ernie and I also were the beneficiaries of this hospitality. The three of us were welcomed to dinner as if it made no difference whether there were seven mouths to feed or ten. Carla is a bright and vivacious hostess, a living example of America's famous "southern charm." We were made to feel like favorite uncles.

Uncles in the Willoughby household have responsibilities, one of which is to tell the bedtime story to five rambunctious boys. Ernie volunteered to do this duty the first night we were there. He told a story from the days when he was an MAF pilot in Africa. It happened that Ernie had a friend back in London, and one day this friend was stopped in a line of London traffic waiting for a red light to change. This friend noticed that the driver of the car ahead of him had a large handlebar mustache that was so wide it could be seen from behind. The friend thought of Ernie, and how Ernie had always hoped that his mustache would grow that wide. Then the friend was led to pray for Ernie in a most urgent way. The friend had no idea exactly where Ernie was or what he was doing at that moment; he only knew that Ernie must be in some great need.

Later that same day the friend wrote to Ernie to tell him how he'd been led to pray for him at that particular time. When Ernie got his friend's letter, he checked his logbook to see where he was at the moment his friend had been praying for him. According to the logbook, he had been flying across Central Africa and had run into low-lying storm clouds. It was impossible to see where to land. He was nearly out of gas. Then, at the very moment of his friend's prayer, he flew into a small opening in the clouds, spied a grass landing strip below, and landed safely with but minutes to spare. As soon as he had landed, the clouds closed in again.

When Ernie had finished his account, one of the boys piped up: "Can we have our story now?" I thought to myself that this new generation had pretty exacting criteria for what constituted a story. When the next night it was suggested that I tell the story, I deferred to Asbjorn. What chance would I have with such a discriminating audience?

We turn now to the second missionary couple we met in Ulan Ude—Pablo and Celeste Ribera. Their story is told in the next chapter.

PABLO AND CELESTE RIBERA

CHAPTER TWELVE

A native Paraguayan with New Zealand citizenship working in Siberia—that surely qualifies one for the title, "World Christian." The only thing missing is a degree from Harvard. And the way Pablo is going, I'd not be surprised to see him correct this lack before long! Celeste is a New Zealander whom he met while she was working as a missionary in Paraguay. They married, and God led them as a couple to Siberia. The ranks of the missionary movement are becoming more and more filled with people like Pablo and Celeste, who call the whole world their home but whose citizenship is in heaven.

There is still a lingering stereotype of the foreign missionary as a frumpy, colorless, ascetic, out-of-touch individual who could never have cut it in his or her own country. I frankly don't think I know a missionary who fits that stereotype, certainly not one under ninety. Missionaries, by the very nature of their calling, are people with guts, grit and savvy, people who push themselves to the limit and, with God's help, accomplish things that others only dream about. In addition, they are up-to-date, "with-it" people who, along the way, produce children who are more likely to make a mark in the world than those of any other profession. If you doubt me, let me introduce you to Pablo and Celeste Ribera, as bright and attractive a couple as I know of, who are in the process of lighting some fires up in the cold vastness of the Republic of Buryatia.

Celeste was born into a Christian home in England in 1961, and her family immigrated to New Zealand when she was four. Originally Anglican, the family switched to an Assemblies of God church in New Zealand that was experiencing revival. Celeste committed her life to Christ at age twelve during a church-sponsored children's camp, and as a teenager she experienced the baptism of the Holy Spirit.

During her late teens, Celeste did not follow the Lord closely; she lived more according to her own will. As she put it, Jesus was still her Savior, but He had ceased to be her Lord. She had a desire to travel, so she went to England and entered nursing school. During that time God spoke to her and told her that she could not live in the world as she had been doing; she must either choose her way or His way. She chose His way.

His way led back to a church in Auckland, New Zealand, where Celeste grew in her faith. She began to sense a call to missions, faintly at first, that became stronger and stronger. She felt that God was taking her natural desire to travel and using it to direct her into a missionary career. She became increasingly interested in South America, and believed that God was leading her to serve there. In this she was encouraged by her pastor and the congregation of her church; with their approval she went to a night Bible school. But by the end of three years in Auckland, Celeste had become quite comfortable living where she was, and she found her desire for missionary service waning.

Then in 1986 God brought a crisis that had the effect of kicking her out of the nest: she lost her job, and with it, all means of supporting herself. Again she turned to her pastor and church, hoping they would send her out as a missionary. But no mission agency seemed interested in her; each one she approached told her that she needed more Bible school, that she wasn't ready to be a missionary, that she needed to "grow up."

Some months earlier Celeste had corresponded with a missionary in Paraguay named Wilbur Blackman, whom she had heard about. One day, unexpectedly, this missionary phoned her in Auckland and asked her to come to Paraguay to help with his mentally handicapped daughter who suffered from juvenile diabetes. Celeste agreed to come, and her church, which had less than a hundred members, agreed to support her. The Falkland War had just ended, and there was a six-month waiting list for flights in and out of Argentina, but Celeste got a seat within a few weeks and at two-thirds the ordinary price. Within a month she was in Paraguay, helping one of the country's best-known missionaries as a nurse, teacher, housekeeper, and cook.

Two years younger than Celeste, Pablo had been born into one of Paraguay's foremost families. Both of his grandfathers had been heroes in the war between Paraguay and Bolivia—essentially an "oil war" between Texaco and Standard Oil. Pablo's mother had inherited a fortune at age twenty-one, and his father had married her for her money. She bore him three daughters, during which time he managed to squander most of her fortune. Then shortly before Pablo's birth his father abruptly left, charging that Pablo was the child of adultery. It was a false charge, but in male-dominated Paraguay the father easily won a divorce. So Pablo's mother, her fortune wasted, was left on her own to raise him and his three sisters.

After five years Pablo's mother married an uncaring Argentinian engineer, and the family settled unhappily in Argentina. The stepfather, though intelligent, could never hold a job; so the family moved from place to place, finally ending up in Sao Paulo, Brazil. A younger brother was born, who was the father's favorite. This brother received the best clothes and was sent to a private school, while Pablo and his sisters were neglected. The four stepchildren felt increasingly ashamed and bitter.

At age fifteen, Pablo started smoking marijuana; by age eighteen he was an addict. During this confused time his mother divorced his stepfather. She found herself unable to provide for Pablo and his sisters. One of the sisters became pregnant and married, another got involved in drugs, and the third disappeared; Pablo has no idea what has happened to her.

During those dark years Pablo felt he was losing his mind. He was afflicted with fear, fear of demons, fear of death, fear, above all, of himself. He desperately wanted to control himself; he feared he might commit suicide, commit a crime. He tried to study. He needed a score of ninety to enter university, but only made eighty-eight. To survive, he got a job. He continued smoking marijuana.

One day Pablo and an acquaintance smoked a "brick" of marijuana, hoping to escape their woes. The acquaintance passed out, but Pablo remained conscious. His life passed before him: his black past, his black present, his black future. And for the first time he prayed to God.

Pablo had always had a vague concept of a remote God, uninvolved in the affairs of men. But this day, in desperation, Pablo called out to this God to see if He would hear him.

"I heard you were a God of forgiveness. Can you forgive me? I heard you were a God of love. Can you love me? I have nothing to offer you: no school diploma, no job, no home, no family, no friends, no money." As Pablo observed to me, he wasn't offering God a very good deal.

God heard Pablo's prayer, and created in his heart a desire to know Him. "No one can come to me unless the Father . . . draws him" (John 6:44).

Pablo moved back to Paraguay to get a new start. He found a job, and his new boss turned out to be a Christian. The boss gave each of his workers a New Testament for Christmas, plus other booklets on the Christian faith. Pablo realized that despite the hard circumstances he had been dealt in life, he himself was a sinner and in need of a Savior. He read Jesus' words: "Come to me, all you who are weary and burdened, and I will give you rest" (Matt. 11:28). ". . . whoever comes to me I will never drive away" (John 6:37).

One day as Pablo was praying in his room, the Holy Spirit descended on him. He felt like he was on fire. He fell to the floor, and cried and cried. He felt engulfed by God's love. He knew he had met with God.

From that moment on, Pablo's life was transformed. The despair, the fear, the loneliness, the addiction—all these were gone. He was twenty-one years old.

Pablo began to devour God's Word. He sought fellowship in the Catholic church, the only church he knew. But what he found there did not agree with what he was reading in God's Word. Pablo wanted to serve God, to give back to God something of what he had been given. His boss suggested a charismatic Protestant church that he himself attended, so Pablo became a member of that church. Its pastor was a missionary named Wilbur Blackman.

Pablo became a church worker. After two years had passed, Pablo received an impression from God that he was to learn English, that for a new life a new language was needed, and that God was preparing for him an English-speaking wife. Furthermore, God impressed upon Pablo that he must keep himself pure, that he must start being faithful to his future wife from now on. Finally, God indicated to Pablo that he would meet his wife-to-be within one year.

Twelve months later Celeste arrived to take care of Pastor Blackman's daughter. God said to Pablo, "This is to be your wife."

Pablo told Wilbur Blackman this, but Wilbur thought he was nuts.

Because of his new faith in Christ, Pablo's mother and other family members had rejected him. He had nothing to offer Celeste, no family, no money, no job, no prospects. But eight months after Celeste's arrival in Paraguay, he proposed. He had one dollar in his pocket and holes in all his clothes.

Celeste had planned to say no. She had even rehearsed the answer "no" in her mind. But she said yes.

Then a week later she came to her senses and said no. From a human standpoint, she just couldn't see the marriage working. And from a human standpoint, she was right.

But what she couldn't see was the spiritual potential for their marriage. God then said to her: "Haven't I looked out for you and Pablo separately until now? Can't you trust me to look out for you together in the future?"

A week later Celeste said yes again, and stuck with it.

Their pastor, Wilbur Blackman, refused to even announce their engagement. He still thought it was nuts.

Meanwhile, Celeste's visa for Paraguay was about to expire, and she was unable to renew it. So she went to England where, according to plan, Pablo was to join her in time for the wedding, which was set for the following July, eight months away.

Pablo, of course, had no money to fly to England. He had no clothes to wear at his wedding. But God impressed on his heart Paul's great statement in Philippians 4:19: ". . . my God will meet all your needs according to his glorious riches in Christ Jesus."

Pablo felt God saying to him, "Pray to me as a Father, and I will give you what you need."

So Pablo wrote down a long list of his needs. He felt he should be specific—size, color, quantity. And within six weeks of the wedding date, Pablo had exactly nothing on his list.

Then Pablo felt God telling him to write a wedding announcement to all his friends and acquaintances, stating that the wedding would be held in England on July 23. Pablo asked himself, "Is this God who is saying this? How can I send these announcements? I have no way of getting to England myself!"

Pablo sent the announcements. Within days, gifts began pouring in. He was given tickets to England. Every single item on his list was given to him—and he had never made the list known to anyone.

After their marriage Pablo and Celeste returned to their former church in Paraguay, where Pablo became an associate pastor. However, they found this church becoming increasingly exclusive; more and more emphasis was being placed on having an "experience" and on shepherding. Pablo and Celeste felt stifled; the church had become a cult. They wanted to leave, but had nowhere to go. They felt spiritually broken.

Finally they gathered up their courage and resigned. They had no idea what they would do or how they would support themselves. Within a week, the pastor of Celeste's former church in New Zealand telephoned them, and said that he and his elders had felt led by the Spirit to urge them to return to New Zealand. Celeste had told her church in New Zealand nothing about their trials in Paraguay; the phone call had come out of the blue—entirely prompted by the Holy Spirit.

After some time in the New Zealand church, Pablo and Celeste were put back on their spiritual feet. They were set free from the deception and false teaching they had been subjected to in Paraguay, and they were healed and renewed through the love of their fellow church members.

Pablo and Celeste had thought their days of ministry were over. But during the next few months they heard about new opportunities in missions. They took a course based on the book, *Perspectives on the World Christian Movement,* a collection of essays on modern missions. And they heard a speaker talk about new openings in places like Mongolia, places that had never been reached with the gospel.

Pablo and Celeste were each individually challenged by the idea of going to Mongolia, but they didn't tell each other at first for fear the one would think the other crazy. Additional information on Mongolia came to them through magazine articles and news broadcasts: everyone, it seemed, was going there. They asked their pastor what he thought about their going there too. He suggested they make a further study of the country and report back to him.

During the course of their study, Pablo and Celeste learned about the Republic of Buryatia, directly north of Mongolia, which contained many unreached people who were ethnically similar to the Mongolians. They asked themselves, "Why should we go to Mongolia, where everyone else is going? Why not go to Buryatia, where no one is going and which no one has even heard of?"

So Pablo and Celeste brought the Republic of Buryatia to the attention of their church. The church agreed in principle to commission them as missionaries to the Buryats. However, the church had recently taken a mortgage, and the elders felt that the church first needed to become financially strong and meet its own needs before getting involved in the needs of a faraway people. They had forgotten that missions was the very purpose of the church; they had relegated it to being an extra—resources permitting. Pablo and Celeste saw no way of going any time soon; it would be years before their church felt ready to support them.

About eighty miles away in the New Zealand town of Tauranga, a group had begun meeting who desired to adopt an unreached people. As a result of seeing a prayer leaflet Celeste had composed about Buryatia, this group decided to make the Buryats their adopted people. So when Pablo and Celeste's own church failed them, God raised up another group to help send them on their way. Shortly thereafter, they were accepted by an international sending agency, which agreed to take care of their travel and oversee their work.

In the final months before their departure, they received further confirmation of their call to Buryatia. They met people who had actually traveled there—even the landlady of the flat they were renting had been there! *National Geographic* during that period ran a twelve-page article on Buryatia. Everything else seemed to fall into place, including a six-thousand-dollar gift just when it was needed. So in the summer of 1994, Pablo and Celeste said their good-byes to their hometown church in Auckland, and journeyed to Buryatia, traveling the last leg of the journey over the rolling grasslands of northern Mongolia on the Trans-Siberian Railroad.

When they reached their destination, everything fell apart. I have not heard a recent missionary story where so many things went so badly wrong. No one met them. The contact who had been arranged refused to see them. A major misunderstanding arose with the government department under which they were supposed to work. They could not get a residence visa. They were running out of money. They knew no Russian. After three weeks in a cheap hotel, Pablo was "going bananas." They thought about leaving. The idea kept tormenting them: "This has all been a giant mistake."

Welcome to the mission field! Not that mission administrators delight in putting new workers through such trials! Far from it. But things can and do go "wrong," despite the best-laid plans. It is not often, however, that everything goes wrong at once.

Is there a happy ending to this story? At their darkest moment

God spoke to them: "You are putting too much importance on arrangements, contacts, visas, money. You are 'under the circumstances' when you should be 'over' them. I am the God of circumstances. Lift your eyes to me."

And Pablo and Celeste did just that. Within days their temporary visa was extended. They met someone who got them a job teaching English. To get a residence visa, they needed a permanent address; to get a permanent apartment they had to pay a full year's rent in advance—twelve hundred dollars. A gift of two thousand dollars came from New Zealand, so they not only got their apartment but were able to furnish it too. Their residence visa was approved.

Today Pablo teaches English in a school in the central part of Buryatia. He and Celeste are serving a church there, which is the only alive and witnessing church for an area the size of Scotland and Wales combined, a single ray of light in a population of 150,000. They are hoping to establish a network of congregations among the Buryat people in their area, and they have imparted this vision to the members of their local church. A light is shining in central Buryatia today, in no small part because Pablo and Celeste were obedient to God's Word and faithful to the vision He had given them.

KALMYKIA

CHAPTER THIRTEEN

Our trip to China, Mongolia, and Buryatia ended up back in Stockholm, Sweden, where I met a most remarkable woman, Anna Larsson, a member of the Swedish Slavic Mission. Anna was in her late fifties when I met her, and had a wide-ranging ministry all over Europe and Asia teaching in Bible schools and discipling young church leaders. In more recent years, God had led her to concentrate her energies on the Tibetan Buddhist world, and this had led to periods of ministry in such far-flung places as Bhutan, Nepal, the Republic of Tuva in Siberia, and finally the Republic of Kalmykia in western Russia.

Anna started her missionary career in the Salvation Army. She felt called to be an evangelist, but she was a shy person, and she didn't see how she could do all the talking that would be required of an evangelist. So she disobeyed God's call, and went to work in the Salvation Army's social welfare department, where she served for four years.

By the end of the four years she had begun to feel increasingly convicted that she was disregarding her calling to evangelism. So one day, during a time of communion with God, Anna determined to move from the social work department and become a full-time evangelist. The very next day after that decision, a Salvation Army leader approached Anna and told her he believed she should be doing evangelism. He had not known of her decision the day before. So Anna left her department to join the evangelistic corps, where she served for another four years before joining the Swedish Slavic Mission in 1971.

Under the Slavic Mission, Anna began her travels in earnest, speaking in churches across northern Europe about the suffering church in Communist countries. Later, with the opening of the former Soviet Union, she began teaching in Russian churches and in the Bible schools her mission had established in various parts of the Soviet block. Under *glasnost* more and more Russian students began coming to Sweden for Bible school, and some of them became Anna's students. One of these students, Sasja, invited Anna to visit his home in Russia, and she did so. While she was there he took her to Kalmykia.

Kalmykia is small republic of Russia located just west of the Volga River as it empties into the Caspian Sea. It is home to nearly 200,000 Kalmyks, who are Lamaistic (Tibetan) Buddhists. Another 150,000 Kalmyks still live in western Xinjiang province, China, their original home. In the early 1600s the Kalmyks, a collection of different Mongol tribes, migrated westward from their homeland and settled in present-day Kalmykia. Then in 1943, Stalin forcibly moved them back to Siberia, to an area just west of Buryatia. They suffered tremendous hardships. Only after Stalin's death were these exiles allowed to return to Kalmykia, where they have since tried to regain their national identity. Though separated geographically from the rest of the Tibetan Buddhist world, the Kalmyks have remained staunchly Buddhist down through the centuries.

Back in Sweden after her visit to Kalmykia, Anna decided to learn Russian, which most Kalmyks speak, and to return to Kalmykia to do her language study. She had also heard that the largest Buddhist temple in all of Europe was being built in Kalmykia. Kalmykia was fast becoming a center for Buddhism worldwide, and Anna felt that that was where she should be.

Before Anna left Sweden, she spoke in her church about her plans to go to Kalmykia. A nearly blind woman who was present came up to Anna afterward and told her of a vision she had had several days earlier. In the vision this woman had seen a huge rock, on top of which were some dried seeds. Then a great rain fell, the rock split, and the seeds sprouted. Then, in the vision, the woman saw someone going as a missionary to that place, and she saw a river of water flowing through the rock that could not be stopped. The woman had not known what that place was, but after hearing Anna, she realized her vision had been about Kalmykia.

The significance of the split rock, however, only became apparent after Anna had arrived in Kalmykia. She found that the Buddhist leaders, the lamas, were divided into two parties, the Buryat lamas and the Kalmyk lamas. These two parties were feuding with each other; the

Kalmyk lamas had even accused the Buryat lamas of stealing money which had been donated for the construction of the new temple. So Anna now knew the meaning of the vision: the rock of Buddhism in Kalmykia had split.

Sometime before Anna left Sweden, the Dalai Lama had appointed a new Rinpoche (chief lama) for Kalmykia, who was considered to be the reincarnation of an Indian guru who had lived several generations before. The new Rinpoche had been chosen from a small Kalmyk community living in New Jersey, USA! He had been trained in South India and in other Buddhist centers, and had only recently been installed as the Rinpoche when Anna arrived in Kalmykia. One of his first acts was to send the troublemaking Buryat lamas back to Buryatia.

Not long after Anna's arrival in Elista, the capital of Kalmykia, she had the opportunity to meet the new Rinpoche. She told him about Jesus Christ, and how He had said He was "the way and the truth and the life" (John 14:6). The Rinpoche politely replied that he had heard all about Jesus and had read the New Testament. They talked together for an hour. When they parted, Anna realized that she hadn't specifically invited the Rinpoche to accept Christ, and she regretted this deeply. She prayed for another opportunity to meet him.

Anna did meet the Rinpoche once more. He was scheduled to give a speech to the Kalmyk people, and Anna was able to speak with him just after the meeting. She shared Christ more openly with him, and urged him to consider Christ's claims. She said she would pray for him. Then it was time to go.

One of Anna's most important colleagues in Kalmykia was a Russian named Ivan, whom she had gotten to know earlier while he was at Bible college in Sweden. Ivan was now living in Elista, and was the pastor of the only indigenous church in Kalmykia.

Ivan had been an ardent Communist and avowed atheist up until the age of eighteen. Then some Russian Christians from Moldavia, who were Gideons, had come to his village and handed out Bibles. Ivan got hold of a copy and began to read it.

Ivan became interested in what the Bible had to say, but he couldn't fully comprehend what he was reading. This frustrated him because, as a university student and self-described intellectual, he felt he should be able to grasp the meaning of any new teaching. But the Bible's meaning eluded him. Not only did he fail to understand its spiritual teaching, he also failed to see how it applied to him personally. Nevertheless, he felt impelled to continue studying the Bible.

Then one day God revealed Himself to Ivan. No longer was this God an impersonal, intellectual concept. He was alive and real. Then, as Ivan was standing alone in his room, he suddenly saw Jesus on the cross. It was an inner revelation in his mind, but it was just as vivid and clear to him as the room in which he was standing. Ivan fell to his knees at the foot of the cross he was seeing in his vision, and he began to weep. Like lightning, the meaning of the Bible was revealed to him, and he understood who Jesus was and what He had done for him—that He had died for Ivan's sins. Ivan then cried out to Jesus, "Forgive me for my sins." Then and there, Ivan experienced God's forgiveness and felt the burden of his sin being lifted away. And in place of that burden he felt his heart being flooded with a joy and peace such as he had never thought possible.

At first Ivan assumed that because he was a Russian, the only way to be a believer was to join the Russian Orthodox Church. But he found the Orthodox churches he visited to be nothing like the church he read about in the New Testament. So he determined to study the Bible and be a believer on his own. But he felt isolated, with no one to turn to for fellowship. So he prayed for God to send him someone who could be his friend and teacher. And God answered his prayer by sending a young American named Jim Morrison.

Jim arrived in Kalmykia in 1988. He had given his life to Christ in high school, and had experienced God's call to foreign missions shortly thereafter. During college, he heard about Kalmykia, and became convinced that that was where God wanted him to go.

Jim's initial priority was to learn the Kalmyk language. To do this, he offered himself as an English teacher and got a job at the university in Elista where Ivan was studying. So Jim became simultaneously a teacher of English and a learner of Kalmyk.

During his early days at the university, Jim met Ivan and immediately befriended him. They began to study the Bible together. Then Jim baptized Ivan. Jim also led five Kalmyk students to Christ during this period.

Then unexpectedly, Jim had to return home to the USA. Ivan was worried about what would happen to the five Kalmyk believers during Jim's absence, so Jim said to Ivan, "You meet with the believers once a week, and teach them just as I have been teaching you."

But Ivan, only eighteen, felt he was too young and too new a Christian to be teaching others. He was embarrassed and hesitant. Nonetheless, after Jim had gone, Ivan did begin to meet informally with the five Kalmyk believers, and God kept giving him new insights that he could then share with the others. So helpful were these insights and so clearly inspired by God, that the five Kalmyk believers asked to have the meetings weekly instead of only occasionally, and soon after they were asking for twice weekly meetings. God continued to give Ivan new thoughts day by day, and all the believers were excited and eager to learn.

These first five believers began bringing their Kalmyk friends to the meetings, and the little group began to expand. When Jim returned from America some months later, the group had grown to fifteen, all of them students at the university. Jim baptized them all.

Thus an infant Kalmyk church came into being. It continued to grow, and one year later it had doubled to thirty members. Since most of the believers were students, many returned to their own villages when their university studies were over, and thus the seed of God's Word was carried all over Kalmykia, with small congregations sprouting up wherever the students settled.

It was during this time that opposition began to grow to this burgeoning Christian work. The chief Russian Orthodox priest heard about it, and did everything in his power to oppose it. In addition, there was a Russian Baptist minister in Elista, who was firmly convinced that the gospel was not meant for the Kalmyks, that they couldn't be saved. He was so upset with Jim's growing church that he notified the KGB. Not long afterward, Jim's permission to stay in Kalmykia was revoked, and he was forced to return to America.

Before Jim left for the final time, he asked Ivan to take over the leadership of the church. Again Ivan protested that he was too young, but eventually he agreed to accept the responsibility for this new flock. And God blessed Ivan's ministry, and He gave Ivan the gifts of teaching and healing.

It became increasingly clear to Ivan that, even though he was a Russian, God had appointed him to be a missionary to the Kalmyks. He started to learn the Kalmyk language. Before that he had been using

Russian, which most of the Kalmyk believers also knew. He married a lovely Kalmyk girl named Sofia, whom he met at the university. And then he heard about the chance to take a formal six-month course at a Bible school in Sweden, and he and Sofia jumped at the opportunity. And so, in 1990, Ivan and Sofia journeyed to Sweden to Bible school, where they became acquainted with Anna Larsson.

Thus it was in God's plan that when Ivan's course was over and he and Sofia had returned to Kalmykia, Anna would then join them there and continue supporting and encouraging them in much the same way Jim Morrison had done earlier. Since then the Kalmyk church in Elista has continued to grow. Ivan has now baptized more than a hundred believers. And together with Jim, still back in America, Ivan is translating the Bible into the Kalmyk language. God has used an American, a Swede and a Russian to build His church among the Kalmyk people, but the chief builder is God Himself.

However, Satan has not withdrawn his opposition to the work. Security agents continue to harass Ivan and others among the believers. Campaigns of slander are still being carried out against them, mainly perpetrated by the Buddhist lamas and also by leaders of the Orthodox church. And perhaps Jim has paid the highest price of all. Shortly after returning to America, he was struck by a drunk driver and severely injured. He is still recovering. The enemy does not sleep.

Most of the above story of the Kalmyk church I heard directly from Anna in June 1996, during my visit to Stockholm on the way home from Mongolia and Buryatia. Anna is a courageous and energetic woman, with a broad grin and a sparkling wit. Anyone who thinks all Scandinavians are dour and humorless ought to meet Anna, and such a notion will quickly be dispelled.

It would also have been dispelled if one had sat in on a meeting I attended in Stockholm made up of mission representatives called to discuss new mission opportunities among the Tibetan Buddhist peoples of Siberia. The participants were mostly Norwegians and Swedes, none of whom would miss a chance to stir up the longstanding rivalry between the two countries. We had hardly sat down for the meeting when a jovial Swede began by telling of a joint Swedish-Norwegian expedition to land the first man on the sun. The Swedish members of the expedition quickly realized it would be impossible; the sun would be too hot. But the Norwegian members said, "It's no problem. We know just how to do it. We shall go by night."

"Ho, ho, ho," laughed the Swede, and a chorus of chuckles went up from the Swedish side of the table.

While the Swedes were still inhaling their last chuckles, my Norwegian friend Asbjorn asked the group, "Do you know why Christ could not have been born in Norway?"

"Why not?" everyone asked.

"Because there are no wise men to the East."

It was the Norwegians' turn to laugh.

After twenty minutes of regaling each other, the participants were ready to get down to business. I concluded that if God could unite Swedes and Norwegians in mission, there was hope for us all.

SNAKES AND DEMONS

CHAPTER FOURTEEN

God calls some Christians to work in a particular country; such was my own case, when I was called to serve in Nepal. Other Christians are called to work among the people of a particular culture or religion. Often, as in the case of Tibetan Buddhism, the culture and religion may be dispersed over a wide geographic area that includes several countries. But some Christians have been called to focus on the ethnic Tibetans themselves. The Tibetans inhabit not only Tibet proper but also much of the high-altitude plateau land of Central Asia. And in addition, as we have already mentioned, tens of thousands of Tibetans have fled their homeland and settled in refugee camps in various parts of Nepal and India.

One such Christian attracted to the Tibetans from an early age was a Norwegian woman named Margaret. When she was seventeen, she met a group of thirty Tibetan refugee girls, who had been brought to Scandinavia to be trained as health workers and secretaries. The Tibetan girls were on an outing in a forest in Norway, and Margaret saw them doing a Tibetan dance and, in her words, she "fell in love with them."

Margaret was not a Christian at the time, but this contact with these Tibetan girls was used by God not only to draw Margaret to Himself but also to draw her to the ministry to which He had called her. That day in the forest in Norway, Margaret made friends with one of the Tibetan girls, whose name was Sangey. After Sangey returned to India to work as a secretary in one of the Tibetan refugee camps, she and Margaret began to correspond with one another in English. Margaret felt more and more attracted to the Tibetan Buddhist religion, and though she had been brought up in a

Christian home, she came almost to the point of accepting Buddhism for herself.

During one exchange, Margaret asked Sangey how she, as a Tibetan Buddhist, received forgiveness. Sangey replied that if one made any mistake a first time, one simply had to perform certain rituals and the mistake would be forgiven. For a mistake committed a second time, one needed to go to the lama. For the same mistake committed a third time, there was no forgiveness.

When Margaret read that, the finality of the prospect of "no forgiveness" frightened her. She had become increasingly conscious of the importance of forgiveness in her own life, and suddenly in Tibetan Buddhism she saw the possibility that forgiveness could be cut off from her forever. Margaret says it was this discovery about Tibetan Buddhism that stopped her from becoming a Buddhist. Instead she gradually returned to her Christian roots, and experienced the eternal and all-encompassing forgiveness offered by God through faith in the Savior, Jesus Christ.

As Margaret's faith deepened, she realized more and more that Christ was not merely her own personal Savior but the Savior of the whole world as well. And if He was the Savior of the world, He also had to be the Savior of Tibetans. As this realization gripped her, she felt led to pray for the Tibetan people and for Sangey in particular. And gradually she felt God calling her to go to the Tibetans and show them that Jesus was their Savior too.

God's missionary call often comes to us when we are young, but then it may be many years before we actually arrive in our place of service. The delay may be legitimate; training and qualifications may be needed, or perhaps there are other commitments to fulfill before going to the field. But sometimes the delay is from our adversary Satan, who desires to thwart God's purpose for our lives. Many of a missionary's greatest spiritual battles occur before he or she ever gets to the field. Such was the case with Margaret.

Margaret decided to train as a nurse. During her training she began to explore possibilities for ministry among Tibetan Buddhist people, but found none. Nurses were needed for many fields, but back in the early 1970s no mission agencies were focusing on Tibetan Buddhists, and none had an established work among them. Mission leaders repeatedly advised Margaret to abandon her notion of working among

Tibetans and instead go to a place where work was already established. Margaret had reason to question whether God was indeed calling her to Tibetan work; perhaps she was just pursuing her own dream and it was not God's will after all that she work among Tibetans. But Margaret did not abandon her vision.

The mission that Margaret initially considered joining wanted her to work in one of their already established fields. As all the other agencies had done, they told her they did not have a field among Tibetan Buddhists. Margaret pointedly asked them, "How can some place become a mission field if no one has ever gone there?"

Then Margaret heard about a mission-run orphanage in the city of Bangalore, located in the southern Indian state of Karnataka. Margaret corresponded with the Indian vicar who ran the orphanage, and learned that there were twenty-two Tibetan children living there. So she decided to go to Bangalore to this orphanage, anticipating that in some way God would open up the opportunity for her to work among Tibetans.

Very soon after arriving in India, Margaret learned that more than 30,000 Tibetan refugees had recently been moved down from northern India to Karnataka state and had been resettled in five refugee camps in a sparsely populated area half a day's drive west of Bangalore. She immediately made inquiries about working in these camps. Since her own mission could not support her in this venture, she decided to become a fully independent missionary and work among these Tibetan refugees on her own. So she left the orphanage in Bangalore and journeyed to the area of Karnataka where the Indian government had resettled the Tibetans. The year was 1980.

Each of the five camps held over a thousand refugees, and in the center of each camp was a hospital. Margaret got a ride to one of the camps and promptly bumped into Sangey, who was working there as a secretary. Margaret had kept in touch with Sangey over the years, and so she knew generally where to look for her. Sangey had married by this time, and her husband happened to be one of the leaders of this particular camp. So he arranged for Margaret to serve in the camp hospital as a nurse, and in this way Margaret's vision for working among the Tibetans became a reality.

All through the 1970s and 1980s, Tibetan refugees trickled south from Tibet, first into North India, and then southward into Karnataka state, where there are today over 100,000 refugees. These refugee camps have maintained and perpetuated the purest form of Tibetan culture to be found anywhere in the world—purer even than that found in Tibet itself, given the great changes wrought there by the Chinese occupation. In the camps exact replicas of Buddhist temples have been constructed, and there the refugees diligently carry out all the required observances of the Tibetan Buddhist religion. Indeed, they show considerable hostility to other belief systems, as Margaret quickly discovered. Only a short time before she arrived, a Christian organization had distributed literature in the camps, and the lamas had ordered that it all be collected and publicly burned. So Margaret remained cautious and discreet as she witnessed about her faith. She kept just one tract on the table in her room, and only if a Tibetan asked for it would she give it. Having waited so long to begin her Tibetan ministry, she didn't want to end it prematurely by getting herself kicked out of the camp for proselytizing.

Within a week of Margaret's arrival at the camp, the "Day of the Devil" was observed. It is believed that on this day the devil has special power to inflict misfortune upon people. The Tibetans in the camp refused to do anything that day for fear that some mishap would befall them. The workers at the hospital refused to go to work; only Margaret and the pharmacist, who had been raised in a Christian orphanage, went to the hospital that day. The Tibetans even refused to tip a glass or cup to drink from it; they drank through a straw instead.

Margaret noticed the power the lamas exercised over the people. Much of the people's religious observances appeared to be performed out of fear of the lamas rather than out of any conviction concerning the meaning of the observance itself. The people almost never dared to question the lamas. Margaret recalls only one instance where a lama's decision was disregarded. A very sick child had been brought to her at the hospital. The child required treatment in a larger hospital, four hours away; there was no hope of survival if the child remained there in the camp hospital. Margaret urged the parents to take their child to the larger hospital. The lama was called in for advice. The lama selected three sticks of different lengths: one stood for sending the child to the large hospital; the second stood for keeping the child in the camp hospital; and the third stood for taking the child home. The lama drew the stick representing "home." Margaret prayed quietly that the parents would choose the large hospital, and in the end they did. Sadly, the child died anyway.

Tibetans usually wear a small cloth amulet tied around their necks with a string. These amulets are thought to offer physical protection to the wearer, and in some sense it may be true. For example, Margaret had many patients who needed injections for tuberculosis. Sometimes even new needles would not penetrate the skin of someone wearing an amulet; it was like giving an injection to a wall. But if the patient removed his or her amulet, the injection could be given easily. This occurred on countless occasions.

The amulets did not always ward off illness; they at times seemed to cause it. Margaret remembers a Tibetan man with severe abdominal pain, who did not respond to any of the medicine Margaret had at her disposal. Finally after many days, Margaret suggested that he remove the amulet he was wearing around his neck; and when he had done so the pain immediately disappeared and did not return. My wife Cynthia had an almost identical experience with one of her Tibetan Buddhist patients in Nepal. It is wise not to scoff at the spiritual power that lies behind these artifacts, whether for good or for evil. It is also important to remember that the power of the Holy Spirit is greater than them all.

After his "cure," the man with the stomach pain took his amulet and nailed it to his gate as a sign that it was now powerless to affect him. Years later, Margaret met that man again in Lhasa; he was not a believer, but he had not forgotten what Margaret had told him about the Spirit of truth who was more powerful than the power behind his amulet. Margaret continues to pray that God will use that experience to eventually bring the man to true faith.

Every worker who labors among Tibetans has noted their seeming resistance to the gospel. Sangey herself has not yet become a Christian, despite her friendship with Margaret over many years. But Margaret knows of at least one Tibetan man who has come to faith as a result, in part, of Margaret's presence in that refugee camp. She had been burdened to pray in particular for one section of the camp. She befriended the wife of a monk living in that section and eventually gave her a Christian booklet. Her husband, who had years earlier heard the gospel from a Swiss couple, read the booklet and was deeply affected by it, enough so that from that time on he ceased carrying out the duties of a monk. Not long thereafter, he came to faith in Christ. Fifteen years later, through additional contacts with Christians, he was baptized, and since then he has been working with David Tsering's radio ministry as the Tibetan speaker broadcasting the gospel message into the interior of Tibet. Margaret's witness was one vital step along his road to faith and service.

After working in that camp for nearly five months, Margaret's Indian visa expired, and she was required to leave India. Two days before she left the camp, however, she had an experience that is common, in one form or another, to most missionaries working in the tropics: she encountered a snake. In this case, the snake was a king cobra and it was in her room. That is, half of it was in her room—the head half.

Margaret's room had two doors; one door opened into a hallway, and the other led directly to the outside. There was an inch of space under both of these doors, and Margaret had been advised early on to nail a board across the bottom of the door leading outside to keep the frogs out; for if frogs got into her room, snakes would follow in to eat them.

So Margaret set a board along the bottom of the outside door and kept it there throughout her stay at the camp. However, she did not nail it down. She often thought to herself, "I ought to nail that board down," but she never did. However, the board served its purpose: no frogs and no snakes came into her room. Until her next to last night in the camp.

Margaret was just getting into bed that night when she spied a three-foot king cobra sliding, not under her outside door, but under her inside door, the one opening to the hallway. She pounded on the wall to alert the person in the next room that she needed help. But the Tibetans seemed to be particularly afraid of snakes. The other occupants of the building, hearing Margaret's pounding and shouting, opened their doors and saw the snake, but none dared come near it. There was a common belief that if anyone killed a snake, that person would sooner or later be killed by a snake. In Margaret's experience, the Tibetans had an inordinate fear of death; it was as if a spirit of death hovered over their communities that affected even the outsiders working there. Only the snake, it seemed, was not paralyzed by fear; it was steadily working its way under Margaret's door.

As it turned out, one of the girls in the building had an Indian boyfriend in her room that night and, being less fearful, he took a stick and struck at the snake's tail, which still remained outside Margaret's door. The stick broke, but the boy picked up the stoutest part of the stick and pressed it down upon the snake's tail to keep it from sliding all the way into Margaret's room. The boy was taking a considerable risk, since the snake at any moment could easily reverse its direction and turn back into the hall and strike at him. The boy shouted to Margaret to kill the snake quickly. Margaret looked around for something to kill it with and saw the board at the base of the other door. Thankful now that she had not nailed it down, she picked it up and began whacking at the cobra's head. The cobra dodged and ducked and writhed ever more angrily, and Margaret struck and struck but was unable to land a telling blow. The boy outside kept yelling, "Hurry, hurry!" The snake thrashed and hissed with greater and greater vehemence.

Finally, when a point of maximum desperation had been reached by all the principals, Margaret landed a blow to the snake's head with the edge of her board, and the drama was over. But instead of the jubilation that Margaret expected, she was greeted with concern and sympathy on the part of her fellow apartment dwellers: they were sure she could not live long, because she had killed a snake.

It had been a very close call. If the snake had bitten either Margaret or the boy, they would surely have died, since they could not have obtained the antivenom serum in time. When Margaret left the camp the following day, the Tibetans' goodbye's were saddened and subdued by their belief that she had but a short time to live.

Margaret spent the next four years moving back and forth between Nepal and India. I first met her in Kathmandu on one of her trips into Nepal. Margaret's main work during this time was preparing literature and radio programming in vernacular Tibetan. She encountered obstacles at every turn. Material that had been laboriously translated was lost; printing equipment malfunctioned; stocks were damaged. Yet over and over the Lord's hand overruled in these difficulties. On one occasion the handwritten manuscripts of eleven recently translated pamphlets disappeared, only to turn up in Moscow six months later. On other occasions Margaret was able to find and preserve literature and tapes that were on the verge of being thrown out. By the end of that four-year period, through prayer and the Lord's enabling, Margaret was able to produce a considerable amount of Tibetan-language literature and also to complete thirty Tibetan radio programs—enough to go on the air in Tibetan.

In 1984, while in Kathmandu, Margaret felt the Lord telling her, "Sell all that you have and follow me." She was not sure what was meant by this, but her closest friend in Kathmandu at the time advised her to do exactly what she felt the Lord was telling her. So she sold everything and went to the town of Mussoorie in northern India, a former British hill station and a center for much Christian work. During her time in Mussoorie, Margaret was able to complete a number of literature projects that she had been engaged in. But the Lord seemed to continue saying to her, "Leave it now, and follow me." Margaret wondered why she should leave the Tibetan work that the Lord had so clearly called her to. What could He mean? Margaret decided that she should return to her home country of Norway and wait for further direction.

As the time of her departure drew near, Margaret made plans to leave Mussoorie on the late evening bus to Delhi and then get a flight from Delhi to Oslo the next day. On the evening in question, her last evening in India, Margaret went to the bus station in Mussoorie. The bus was slow to fill up, and since many Indian buses don't leave until they are full, this bus's departure was delayed. As Margaret was standing there outside the bus, she noticed a taxi nearby, also waiting to fill with passengers. There was a seat left in the taxi, and Margaret decided to take it; this way she would be able to leave without further delay and have a more comfortable ride as well. Furthermore, it was considered improper for unescorted women to ride the last bus in the evening. However, the Lord seemed to be telling her, "Get on the bus." Margaret argued with the Lord, giving Him several good reasons why she should take the taxi instead.

Still arguing, she headed for the taxi and bumped—almost literally—into a Westerner walking toward the bus, who introduced himself as Brian Woods. Brian urged Margaret not to take the taxi, but to join him and take the bus, which she did.

On the bus Margaret and Brian discovered that they shared a mutual interest in ministry to the Tibetans. Brian was a photographer for a Christian organization working in Asia and was on assignment in northern India. They spent most of the bus ride talking; before they parted, they exchanged addresses.

The following year, the spring of 1985, Tibet opened to foreigners, and Margaret and a friend made plans to go. They stashed over forty pounds of literature in two bags, covered them with a few clothes, and journeyed to Tibet. As they travelled around the country, they were repeatedly searched at the numerous checkpoints they had to pass through, but not once was their literature discovered. At one checkpoint a German woman in line ahead of them had her roll of toilet paper unrolled as the officer searched for contraband material. When Margaret's turn came, the officer reached into her bag, encountered pamphlets, and pulled one out. But what he pulled out was not a pamphlet but a tourist map that Margaret had stuck in the midst of her other literature. The officer gave back her map and didn't search further.

During the time Margaret was in Tibet, Brian was planning a trip to Tibet himself. He had been asked by his organization to produce a special issue on Tibet for the organization's magazine. One of Margaret's supporting groups, learning of Brian's trip, asked him to take some money to Margaret, which he was happy to do. So Margaret and Brian met once again, this time in Lhasa. And Margaret knew right then that he was the man for her.

That trip to Tibet also reconfirmed Brian's call to Tibetan ministry. In 1988 he and Margaret were married. They have since established a base in an Asian city, from which they have been coordinating ministry efforts in Tibet, chief among them being a ministry of prayer.

In 1990, Brian and Margaret led their first prayer team to Lhasa, and it has been followed over the years by eleven other prayer trips lasting between ten and sixteen days each. Before each trip the teams spend several days in spiritual preparation, prayer, and planning, as they seek the Lord's leading as to what particular strategies should be employed. Each team's overall goal is to see the lordship of Christ established throughout Tibet, and the team's prayers are focused on this goal.

In addition to leading the prayer teams, Brian and Margaret publish prayer guides containing constantly updated information concerning major prayer needs. These prayer guides are distributed to thousands of individuals, groups, and churches around the world. Recently, through Brian and Margaret's efforts, God has raised up over a thousand individuals and churches who have committed themselves to pray intensively for Tibet.

I recently had the chance to visit the Woods' home in their Asian city; there I was able to meet Brian for the first time and to renew my acquaintance with Margaret. I asked Brian about how God had originally called him to serve in Asia.

He said he had been brought up as a Christian; his father had been a minister in the Church of England. When the father retired from active ministry, he moved his family to Australia, where Brian got drawn into drugs. At the age of twenty Brian experienced a dramatic encounter with the Lord, which utterly changed his life. He was rescued from drugs.

Brian then moved to New Zealand, where for five years he devoted himself to the work of his local church. He then studied for three years in a Bible college in Auckland. Brian says: "I had an Anglican background, a charismatic conversion, and an evangelical Bible school; I was prepared for international missions!"

During his last year in Bible college in Auckland, Brian served as the school prayer convener. He was responsible for arranging four special days of prayer during the year, and for making sure that any information or displays on a given prayer topic were in order.

On one occasion, the prayer topic was missions. As Brian was checking the display for that session, he noticed a quotation of Francis Xavier: "Tell the students to give up their small ambitions and come eastward to preach the Gospel of Christ." It was a great quote, Brian thought, and could be used effectively to get others to go into missions.

Many students were blessed through that day of prayer. Some were convicted; others felt called to the mission field. But afterward, Brian himself remained depressed and confused. Everyone seemed to have heard from God but himself! He asked the Lord, "What do you want me to do?"

That week a brochure came in the mail from a mission organization in Asia listing various personnel needs, among them the need for a photographer—a need Brian was equipped to meet. Inside the brochure was that same quotation from Francis Xavier. Other confirming signs quickly followed, and within eight months Brian was on the field working as a photographer.

During the prayer trips into Tibet, Brian and Margaret have had numerous opportunities to witness personally to people they meet and to encourage others who have been witnessed to earlier. On one of Brian's last trips into Tibet, the team he was leading decided to visit a monastery whose monks practiced the ancient Bon religion of Tibet, which predated the advent of Buddhism. When the early Buddhists arrived in Tibet, they accommodated this ancient religion and adopted some of its practices and beliefs, especially its demonology. Buddhism eventually prevailed, of course, but there are still two monasteries in Tibet where the ancient Bon religion continues to be practiced. One of these monasteries was the focus of Brian's prayer team.

On this visit, while Brian was talking inside the monastery with some of the monks, the other team members remained outside praying. Two of them, however, ventured into a temple adjacent to the monastery, challenging the spiritual forces, as it were, on their own territory.

As the team members were walking back to their vehicle after the visit, one of the two women who had entered the temple described the intense spiritual oppression she had experienced inside. The other woman related how she had seen some kind of demonic force holding her companion by the shoulders. She described in detail how this demon had appeared to her: "The demon had a snake in its mouth, and its feet had talons like those of an eagle." And she described many other features of this demon.

As he listened, Brian was strongly led to have the team stop right there on the path and celebrate Communion. They did so, and they prayed against the power of this demon; and the woman who had felt the oppression was released. The next day, the team reached the famous Tashilhunpo Monastery in Xigaze, and there to their amazement they saw, prominently displayed, a statue of the precise demon the woman had described, right down to the last detail. The demon of that ancient Tibetan religion had become a "guardian" of modern Tibetan Buddhism.

Some years ago Brian was in Tibet with a Swiss friend. They had reached a high point where they could look out over a vast area of wild, arid, mountainous landscape. Brian asked his friend pessimistically, "How are these Tibetan people ever going to be reached?" Both of them felt their faith was under attack. So there on that high ground, with Tibet laid out before them, they sang "Worship His Majesty." They felt their faith increase and their oppression lessen, as they once more claimed that land for Jesus Christ. Brian's final words to me as I left his home were: "Never forget the power of worship and praise in spiritual warfare." Brian knows what he is talking about.

From the beginning of Brian and Margaret's ministry among Tibetans, the three pillars of their work have been praise, prayer and proclamation. These would be three essential ingredients of any missionary endeavor.

NARROW ALLEYWAYS AND OPEN DOORS

CHAPTER FIFTEEN

Some of those working among Tibetan Buddhists in various parts of Asia live under constant surveillance. Their phones are tapped; their apartments are bugged; their every move is watched. Recently I met with Bob and Thelma Bridges in an Asian city of several million people. After supper in their apartment, I asked them to share with me their story about how God had brought them to this place and what He was doing through them. They happily agreed to tell me. But first, knowing their room was wired, they put on a tape of classical music to blur our voices—Chopin, as I remember. So as you read this chapter, play some Chopin and imagine the walls have ears, and you'll get a taste of what life is like for those who work in these difficult places. For Westerners who value their privacy, such electronic intrusion is especially burdensome.

Bob had felt God's call to overseas service during college in the USA. After college he studied for one year at Gordon-Conwell Seminary. The following summer he went to India on a missions training program. Bob had always felt drawn to Asia, in part because of the stories he had heard from his father, who had been stationed there during World War II. Bob's summer in India served to increase his interest in Asia even further.

The following year Bob entered a Ph.D. program in agricultural economics and land management. Not long thereafter Bob and Thelma met and, after a whirlwind courtship, married. During those years of study they were constantly encountering Asians: they shared a house with an Asian couple; Bob's advisor was Asian. Bob and Thelma joined the Asian Students Association and became the only non-Asian members. All during the years of postgraduate study, the call to service in Asia become stronger and stronger for both of them.

As Bob and Thelma prayed about where they should serve, they independently came to the conclusion it should be Nepal. However, when Bob's studies were over and it was time to go, there were no openings for them in Nepal. But then the opportunity came for Bob to do research at a university in another Asian country (which shall go unnamed), and both he and Thelma felt clearly that this was God's direction for them. And step by step, God opened the doors for them to move to that university and settle in an apartment on the campus. It was in that same apartment five years later that I met with them to get their story for this book—with Chopin playing in the background.

Bob and Thelma arrived in their country in 1992. They have not had an easy time. The first two years were particularly difficult. Bob found himself in an academic situation for which he was overtrained. Worse, his fellow professors did not appreciate his contribution; indeed, they looked down on him. They couldn't understand why a highly qualified American Ph.D. would come to their out-of-the-way provincial university in the first place; why hadn't he sought a more prestigious post in the West? In their view there were only two possible explanations: either he couldn't make it in the West, or he had an ulterior motive for coming to their country. Perhaps he was a spy—or equally bad, an advocate for some religious sect.

Whichever of these views they held, Bob's colleagues remained cool towards him—indeed, at times, disrespectful. This coolness was especially hard on Bob, because he is a "people person," and enjoys developing good relationships with his colleagues. The worst blow came during his first year in the country when some of Bob's fellow professors met in his apartment to discuss the research he had embarked upon. They questioned him for about an hour, and then finally realized that Bob's research was not going to directly benefit them. One of them abruptly said to Bob, "Well, we shouldn't be taking any more of your time." And then, as a body, they arose and walked out the door without even saying good night—in that culture a gross breach of etiquette. And this unfriendly attitude on the part of Bob's national colleagues remained basically unchanged for Bob and Thelma's first three years in the country.

Adding to Bob and Thelma's frustration and heartache in the beginning was the fact that they had little opportunity for contact with the ethno-religious minority group they had been particularly called to serve— the Lamaistic (Tibetan) Buddhists of the Central Asian highlands.

During their first year in the country Bob and Thelma were so discouraged—even depressed—about their situation that they considered quitting. They thought the leaders of the agency that had sent them must have been nuts to think there was any ministry possible for them in that place.

Then one day Bob found himself walking along a dark, narrow alleyway in the city, with high walls on either side. After some minutes he came out onto a large open area with trees and grass and the sun shining down. And Bob felt the Lord saying to him, "Your life so far has been a dark, narrow alleyway; but you are about to come into a wide, sunlit area. Don't quit now." Bob took this thought as a direct encouragement from the Lord—though he had no idea how the Lord was going to bring him into the "wide, sunlit area."

Thelma was equally frustrated by the lack of contact with the Tibetan Buddhist minority group she had been especially called to. She found herself complaining to God about this lack of contact and about the agency leaders who had not foreseen it. But then she repented of her complaining spirit and asked God to forgive her. A week later she received a phone call asking her if she could teach English to some Tibetan students! She was more than happy to do so.

For Bob also, the opportunity soon came to teach computer science to some of the minority students, including Tibetans. Within a short time four of his students had accepted the Lord—one right after another. No longer could Bob and Thelma claim they had no ministry among the minority people they had come to serve.

Bob and Thelma taught these minority students for two and a half years. Even those who did not believe in Christ became their good friends. These students would visit Bob and Thelma in their apartment and offer them help in practical ways, even long after their particular class had finished. One time Thelma became ill and had to be hospitalized. Conditions in the hospital were not good, and Thelma's illness was slow to respond. But she was greatly encouraged by her Tibetan students, who came to the hospital to visit her bringing fruit and flowers. When at last Thelma recovered, one of her Tibetan students said, "Your God must have made you better." That was the first time any of her students had mentioned God.

One of the Tibetan girls invited Thelma to teach English in her own home village, a twelve-hour bus ride from the university. In order to arrange this teaching opportunity, Thelma went with the girl to her village and spent a week talking to officials and making preparations. During that time Thelma lived with the girl's family.

But shortly after Thelma's arrival in that village the provincial police learned that a foreigner was living with a Tibetan family, and they called Thelma in and told her she was breaking the law by living with nationals. The chief of the provincial police then said to Thelma, "According to the rules, you should be expelled from the village. However, I am not going to deal with your case; instead, I will turn you over to the jurisdiction of the local village police."

So Thelma was taken to the local police station, and when the policemen heard the charges against her, they said, "Aren't you going to be our new foreign teacher?"

Thelma answered, "Yes."

They told her, "In that case, you can stay anywhere you like in our village."

The police were not the only hurdle that Thelma and her village friend had to overcome. Thelma needed a permit to teach in the village, and to obtain this she had to see the Public Security Officer. On the way to his office Thelma passed a bookstall and noticed a book titled *Three Brothers Mountain*. For some reason the book appealed to her and she decided to buy it as a present for Bob. But then she thought better of her impulse—the book held no meaning for her, after all— and she proceeded along the street. But the Lord seemed to say to her, "Go back and buy that book." And so she returned to the stall and bought it.

When she met with the Public Security Officer, he was hardly encouraging. "We've never had a foreign teacher here before," he said. "I don't see how I can issue you a permit."

Then he spied the book Thelma had bought. "Show me that book," he said. And when he had looked at it, he said, "This book is about my home district. I know most of the people and places mentioned here." Then he showed the book to the other people in his office, and they spent a full twenty minutes turning the pages, looking at the pictures, and commenting on what was written.

At the end of the time, the Public Security Officer said to Thelma, "You have my permission to teach here. I'll do all that I can to help you." And he kept his word.

Thelma had many interesting experiences during that first visit. The village had a public shower, which one had to pay a small fee to use. The first time Thelma availed herself of this facility, the place seemed to fill quickly with other women. But they had not come to bathe; they had paid their money to watch Thelma bathe. Such was the novelty of having a foreigner in their village.

The following summer, Bob and Thelma together were able to follow through on Thelma's initial visit and go back to that same village to teach English. While there, Bob and Thelma, along with a few Tibetan friends, visited an ancient Tibetan Buddhist temple located nearby. As they walked around inside, the Tibetans in the party spun each of the large prayer wheels as they passed, but Bob and Thelma did not. After a while one of the Tibetans asked Bob, "Why do you not turn the prayer wheels? Would it displease your God?"

And Bob answered, "Yes, it would. God hears our prayers directly; we don't need such things as prayer wheels. Prayer is really a conversation with the living God."

After Bob and Thelma's summer in that village was over and they had returned to the university, Thelma learned of a small prayer group in Europe that for six years had been praying that God would send someone to that same village. Bob and Thelma were the answer to those prayers.

Bob's involvement with that Tibetan village led to a further opportunity to work with the minority Buddhist peoples of that region. Because of his experience in the village, he was chosen by the university to lead a research project in a nearby area. This project continued for three years until it was terminated by the police, who had been instructed to keep all Americans out of Tibetan areas—except for tourists. A government official even brought false charges against Bob, saying that he was a spy for the U.S. government. But the university came to Bob's defense and rebuked the official for slandering their researcher, and eventually the charges were dropped.

In spite of Bob and Thelma's rewarding work with Tibetan Buddhists out in the field, the coolness and hostility with which Bob was regarded by his fellow professors at the university remained unchanged. At one point toward the end of Bob's second year at the university it became necessary to vacate their apartment temporarily, and so he and Thelma decided to move all their things to Bob's office up six flights of stairs in another building. None of his fellow faculty members offered to help, though many were young and strong. So Bob went to the Foreign Affairs Officer of the university to ask for assistance; but the officer was uninterested, and merely said, "Get yourself a van."

Since a van was not easy to come by in Bob and Thelma's city, he started carrying the contents of their apartment up to his office. Early in the moving process, however, Bob's back began giving out. And so he prayed earnestly to God that somehow he might be provided with a van. Within an hour of that prayer there was a knock on their apartment door, and there stood several Tibetan students from the village where he and Thelma had taught English the previous summer. They had just driven into the city—a twelve-hour drive—in a van!

They were, of course, delighted to help move Bob and Thelma's things. They all pitched in, filled the van, drove to the other building, and carted the stuff up the six flights of stairs to Bob's office. When the job was finished and the Tibetans had gone, Bob went back to the Foreign Affairs Officer and said to him: "Well, I prayed to God for help, and He sent some Tibetans with a van from a village a day's drive from here. I thought you'd like to know."

The officer did not receive this news with pleasure. He remained sullen; he had been humiliated. It was his job to assist the university's foreign personnel, and he had failed to do so. God had raised up some Tibetans to do it for him.

One morning in the fall of 1995 after three years at the university, both Bob and Thelma independently received a clear sense from God that "something has changed." They had no idea what it was, until Bob went to work that day. The university laboratory in which Bob worked had a new director; Bob had a new boss. This new director had a totally different attitude toward Bob than the previous director had. He gave Bob a new office and a new, higher quality computer, and he increased his research money. And, above all, he extended to Bob both his friendship and his respect.

When Bob expressed some amazement at the change, the new director said, "For three years you have been treated badly by the people at this university. From now on, we are going to help you and work with you. You have courage. It's not easy to live here with your family; the USA is much nicer. Our people lack courage, but you have set us an example of courage. I want you to stay. We want to work with you."

While Bob and Thelma were having their ups and downs during those first three years, their three older children were not without ups and downs of their own. Their eldest daughter, Charlene, went part time to a national school nearby. Two of her teachers, the music teacher and the physical education teacher, manifested a disdain for foreign students and repeatedly made derogatory comments about them and about Charlene in particular. Discipline seemed harsh; Charlene would be made to stand in class for long periods for the slightest infraction—even for sneezing. The situation became so bad that Bob and Thelma and a couple of their expatriate colleagues sat down one Sunday morning and prayed that those two teachers would either leave or be changed. That very week the music teacher was fired and the physical education teacher came to Charlene and apologized—an extraordinary act, given the culture of his country. And he did change, and from then on went out of his way to be nice to Charlene.

Bob and Thelma described other instances of God looking out for their children. At one point during their first year at the university, Bob was troubled that his three-year-old son Peter had no playmates. There were very few foreigners in the city, and the children of the national faculty members did not mix with foreign children. One day, riding his bicycle to the store, Bob thought to himself, "There are several million people in this city whom I can't talk to. Where will I find a friend for Peter?" And as he rode, he prayed that God would provide Peter with a friend.

At the store Bob made his purchases, but then he lingered for some minutes, idly looking at the shelves of merchandise. Then as he was about to leave, he noticed a Western woman enter with a small boy in tow. Bob introduced himself, and discovered that the woman was the wife of a foreign consular official in that city. And her son was three years old—exactly Peter's age. This meeting gave little Peter not only a friend but also access to the consulate's pool and playground. And the two little boys became the best of pals.

Toward the end of the evening, as I sat with Bob and Thelma in their apartment listening to their story, I asked them if they had any words of wisdom for other prospective workers thinking to come to their country. Bob said, "The thing I'd emphasize is: Don't be a quitter. Jesus never promised us things would be easy. Even in that first year when all my colleagues walked out on us without a good-bye, even when they thought I was either a dope or a spy, I felt God's presence leading us, urging us forward. And then God began giving us those special signs of His grace—those answers to prayer—to encourage us and to sustain us."

Bob then told me of another expatriate couple who had earlier come to that same city. This couple was ideally suited for the work there: they had the exact professional qualifications needed and, above all, they already were highly proficient in the language. But the husband, in particular, felt he needed a satisfying and fulfilling job in which he could put to use his professional skills. And no such job materialized. Bob suggested to the couple that God might have other plans for them that were more crucial spiritually. He told them of the opportunities that God had opened up for him and Thelma to work among the minorities—the very people this couple also wanted to reach. But they said, "We don't consider such opportunities a 'proper job.'" And so, when a proper job showed no signs of appearing, they left the country and returned home—a great loss to the work.

Bob then commented: "Many new workers are coming out with a nine-to-five mentality. They look for job satisfaction first of all. They don't have a pioneer spirit. They are not willing to be led by God down unexpected paths."

Bob continued: "God wants to test us, to refine us, to bend us. Yes, there will also be a breaking—just the right amount in the place where we need to be broken. In the early years Thelma and I had to keep asking ourselves: Are we ready for God's hand? Do we want to be fully fruitful for Him? Do we want to hear Jesus say at the end: 'Well done'? Then don't quit. Change direction, yes. Endure, yes. Suffer, yes. But quit, no. In the end, we want to be able to say with Paul: 'I have finished the race.'"

In this new day of missions many Christians, like Bob and Thelma, are going out to the field as professionals. But in some instances they are not really wanted by their national colleagues; only their money is wanted. It is almost impossible to meet the nationals' expectations under such circumstances. The nationals are disappointed; it is hard to make friends with them. They suspect the motives of the foreign worker. All of these obstacles the devil uses to try and discourage the worker— and all too often he succeeds.

Added to this is the problem that ministry opportunities are likely to be limited, certainly in the beginning. Some workers go out feeling a call only to a particular people group, and they are frustrated if they can't have sufficient contact with that group. But God is not limited in His thinking to this group or that. If a new worker goes to Bob and Thelma's country, he or she needs to be ready to witness to all people, not just to one particular minority group. As Bob and Thelma did, workers need to pray for contacts, for opportunities, for open doors; and that is always a prayer that God is more than ready to answer—as Bob and Thelma's experience has proven.

RALPH AND RHONDA ATKINS

CHAPTER SIXTEEN

After spending the night in a clean but inexpensive hotel in Bob and Thelma's city, I flew the next day to a remote city in Central Asia, elevation 7,500 feet, located at the edge of the high arid plateau land that is home to the majority of the world's Lamaistic (or Tibetan) Buddhists. Springtime had come to the city, and the bright green leaves of thousands of newly planted roadside trees provided relief from the otherwise barren, orange-brown landscape. About a third of the people were Buddhists, the remainder being adherents of other Asian religions. Though the city was bustling and quite new in appearance, it clearly had not yet experienced the phenomenal economic growth and modernization taking place in other cities of Asia.

A large, recently built hotel in the center of town was to be my home for the next five days. From there I could get a Number 2 bus that would take me from one end of the city to the other, to within walking distance of each of the workers in that city whom I wanted to interview. Like many Asian hotels, this hotel did not give you the key to your room; each time you left your room and locked the door, you had to ask one of numerous, smartly uniformed young ladies to escort you back to your room and let you in. This was not as inconvenient as might be supposed, since there were always half a dozen such young ladies on every floor, waiting to serve the hotel guests. I had come to a labor-intensive society, where it was evidently more economical to provide a woman to open your door than to give you a key.

I had been warned about pickpockets in this city. They were particularly troublesome on the Number 2 bus route, I was told. After many years of living abroad, I had learned to guard my back pocket, and habitually kept my left hand on my wallet, especially in a crowd. But there are always those split seconds when you have to sneeze, or get your glasses out, or pay the conductor; and during one such split second standing in the aisle of the Number 2 bus on my way to my first interview, I felt someone unbuttoning the button of my back pocket.

Reflexly I swung my elbow with considerable force into a burly young man standing behind me, connecting nicely with his mid-epigastrium. He had gotten the button undone, all right, but that was all. He staggered backward, coughing and sputtering, unbalancing several other people in the aisle. I pointed to the young man and said in English, loudly enough for most of the bus to hear, "Thief! Pickpocket!" I'm sure he understood my meaning, though I couldn't tell if anyone else on the bus did. I pointed to my wallet and then again to the young man. Everyone eyed me with a stony, inscrutable expression. Were they upset that I had interfered with the young man's livelihood? At the next stop he got off; and at the following stop, I did too, leaving the passengers sitting as expressionless as before.

My destination was the apartment of Ralph and Rhonda Atkins and their two small children. Ralph was Canadian and Rhonda was from the States. Ralph was a teacher at one of the universities in the city, and the family lived in faculty housing on the campus. The interview was a lively affair, punctuated by the exuberance of Ralph and Rhonda's two children, a visit by the Foreign Affairs Officer of the university, the visit of another friend, a couple of phone calls, and the hopping to and fro of a pet baby rabbit, which I came close to trampling more than once. The most urgent interruption, however, was the sound of liquid pouring off the kitchen stove onto the floor: the milk had boiled over. It brought back memories of the countless similar episodes my wife and I had endured in Nepal over the years. I was able to suggest something we had found invaluable in Nepal: a little glass disk one can set in the milk pot and which clatters audibly as soon as the milk begins to boil. Though the clatter is not loud, it is sufficient—like the rattle of a rattlesnake—to break through all other distractions and focus the mind. I was grateful that my visit could be of at least some potential usefulness.

During his high-school years Ralph had joined a singing group, in which were a number of Christians who met periodically for prayer. Ralph had wondered what went on at these prayer meetings, so one day he decided to attend. During the meeting one of those present, a young black man named Duane, prayed to receive Christ into his life. A week later Duane came down with pneumonia and within a few days was dead. At his funeral service Ralph's group sang. Later, as Duane's body was being lowered into the ground, Ralph felt God say to him: "If Duane had not heard of me, he would not be with me now." That was Ralph's first real evangelistic call. From then on the urge to share his faith never left him.

At university Ralph majored in theological studies with a minor in missions. The theological faculty was decidedly liberal, and Ralph's faith was sharpened and strengthened by constant debate with his teachers. During his university years Ralph was discipled by a Campus Crusade for Christ staff worker, and under his guidance Ralph learned what it meant to walk with Christ in obedience and in the Spirit.

During his first summer at university, Ralph heard a performance by a Christian singing group, the Continental Singers. After the concert, the group invited Ralph to try out. He did so—and he was accepted for a singing tour the following summer. He had a choice of four tours, one of which was to China. Ralph felt God say to him: "China."

So in the summer of 1981, between his sophomore and junior years at university, Ralph went with the Continental Singers to China. He remembers walking down a main street in Shanghai in the midst of a sea of people, and thinking, "These people don't know Christ." After their last concert in Beijing, Ralph was helping to take down the set when an old man came up to him and whispered in his ear, "I am a Christian; thank you for coming." Ralph felt that those words sealed his vision and call to serve God in China.

During his junior year at university Ralph joined a student prayer group, which used *Operation World* as a prayer guide. During each meeting the group prayed for laborers to go out to the various countries that were prayed for. Today every member of that original prayer group is either on the mission field or otherwise totally involved in missions. As Ralph observed to me: "It's very dangerous to pray for laborers!"

The following summer Ralph returned to China, where he spent some weeks at a large university for students from China's ethnic minority groups. There Ralph came into contact with Tibetans for the first time, and he was drawn to them. During that summer and throughout his final year of university, Ralph felt that God was taking his original call to China and focusing it on the Tibetans living in that land. And through prayer and reading, this Tibetan calling became progressively more settled in Ralph's mind.

After university, Ralph went to Central Asia as a full-time language student to learn Mandarin. Ralph had decided he should learn Mandarin before tackling the Tibetan language. During this period of language study he made two trips to Lhasa, where his vision for Tibetan ministry was confirmed and refined. On the second trip to Lhasa, he taught English for one semester, and during that time he encountered some of the difficulties associated with Tibetan ministry—the physical hardships, the spiritual oppressiveness, the illnesses.

Something else happened during Ralph's second year of Mandarin study: he met his future wife Rhonda. Rhonda had come out to the city where Ralph was studying on a summer ministry trip, and there they met and fell in love. Rhonda was a nurse, and she had felt a call to overseas ministry ever since her nursing school days. She had come to believe that belonging fully to the Lord meant she should be willing to serve Him even in the most difficult and faraway places of the world.

However, Rhonda's parents—especially her father—were opposed to her going overseas. Although her call to foreign service was still strong, she decided to defer to her parents' wishes. She realized that she could be fully active in foreign missions right in her own home city of Chicago.

But shortly after making this decision to stay at home, Rhonda was given a pamphlet describing a summer ministry opportunity in Central Asia. She asked permission from her father to go, and he said yes. And it was on that trip that she met Ralph.

When Rhonda got back to Chicago and told her parents she was in love with Ralph, her father was strongly opposed to their getting married. He didn't want his daughter marrying someone who was going to be always "asking for money"—who wasn't a "working man," as he put it. It wasn't that Rhonda's father was opposed to Christian service; he himself was a believer. But he was afraid that Rhonda would somehow suffer if she ended up the wife of an overseas worker, and he didn't want to see that happen.

Nevertheless, in spite of her father's opposition, Rhonda decided to accept Ralph's proposal of marriage; and the following summer, 1986, Ralph returned from Central Asia to marry her. It was only many years later that Rhonda's father came to accept her marriage and her calling to Central Asia. Just recently he told her that it was seeing her surren-

der to the Lord's will that had changed his mind. It wasn't her commitment that made the difference; he had always seen her "commitment"
simply as a part of her struggle against him. But when he saw that she
had truly surrendered her will to the Lord, then he himself felt led to do
likewise. Just a year before my visit to their apartment, Rhonda's father had phoned her and said, "I have laid you on the altar; I have given
you up to the Lord."

As I listened to Rhonda's story, I was reminded of my own parents, and how long it had taken them to become fully reconciled to my
desire to serve God in Nepal. It was only after my parents came to visit
us in Nepal that they saw the life God had given us was indeed rich and
full and worthwhile; and partly as a result of that visit they found their
own spiritual lives renewed and greatly deepened.

Rhonda was twenty-seven when she married. Before that, she had
felt very close to the Lord. But during the tumult of courtship and the
early days of marriage, she lost that sense of closeness to Christ. Now
she was no longer following only the Lord, but she had to follow her
husband as well. Though she had always felt called to overseas service,
she was not at all sure she had been called to Central Asia, much less to
Tibetans specifically. Yet that was now where she was headed. Whose
leading was she to follow?

Gradually Rhonda sensed that the Lord was telling her to follow
her husband. She struggled with that for a time, but then came to realize that her husband was following the Lord, after all, and that if he
kept following Him, then she could trust his leading. Thus she received
a clear call to follow her husband—who was himself following the
Lord. And she learned to pray that her husband would remain a man of
God's Word and continue to walk in obedience to Him. And over time,
as she prayed in this manner, she herself came to deeply love Tibetans
and to genuinely share in Ralph's ministry to them. And today it is
truly a ministry they share equally together.

Following his marriage to Rhonda, Ralph studied for a master's
degree in Teaching English as a Second Language (TESL) at a U.S. university. While he was there, the Dalai Lama came to speak, and Ralph was
impressed by the large number of supporters the Dalai Lama had gained in
the West. Tibetan Buddhism has indeed been attractively dressed up to appeal to Western tastes; but underneath, the core religion remains unchanged,
and it is something quite different from what Westerners suppose.

In 1990 Ralph completed his master's degree, and the couple, together with their first child, returned to Central Asia. Since then they have lived in a number of cities with large Tibetan populations. Ralph has taught English to university students, and on the side he has been learning the northern, or Amdo, dialect of the Tibetan language. And the couple has added a second child to the family—a little Chinese girl whom they adopted near the end of their first term of service.

Along the way, Ralph and Rhonda have made some deep and lasting friendships among the Tibetans they have met. Indeed, Ralph's best friend is a Tibetan. Ralph met this friend several years ago at one of the universities where Ralph was teaching. They began to teach each other their respective languages. Then Ralph visited his friend's home in a remote area of the Central Asian highlands and stayed there for several weeks. During his visit he learned from his friend's father something of the terrible persecution and hardships the Tibetans have endured in recent years at the hands of the majority people. As Ralph and his friend sat listening on the *kang*, the raised, heated platform found in many Tibetan homes, the father related how his own father had been massacred, along with many others. As the father described the ordeal of his people, tears welled up in his eyes.

Ralph's Tibetan friend had a younger brother who was a monk and lived in a monastery with several hundred other monks. One time, Ralph's friend took him to visit his brother in the monastery. There Ralph met an older monk, who immediately wanted to know if Ralph had come to "change our religion." When Ralph's friend said no, the old monk became relaxed and friendly. After a long conversation the old monk mentioned to Ralph that his knees were aching, and so Ralph gave him some Tylenol that he had with him. Later that night at his friend's home, Ralph prayed that the old monk's knees might be healed. The next day he received a note from the monk saying that his knees were now fine.

A few weeks later Ralph again visited that old monk. The monk welcomed him, and at once introduced him to the other monks present, saying, "This is my friend; he believes in Jesus, but that's okay." For Ralph, this was one of many experiences that have convinced him that only by showing love to Tibetans in practical ways can their trust be gained and their hearts won. Those working with Tibetans must prove their friendship and love by acts of service.

During these past few years, both Ralph and Rhonda have been studying a major Tibetan dialect as full-time students. Their new Tibetan teacher has also become a good friend. During the language lessons they talk about many subjects, including religion. Ralph and Rhonda are constantly dependent on the Holy Spirit to help them hold that fine balance between telling the truth and keeping their teacher's friendship.

Witnessing to Tibetans requires great patience. Their world-view is utterly different from that of the gospel. For one full year Ralph and Rhonda's current Tibetan teacher had insisted that Christianity and Buddhism were really the same. Finally Ralph told their teacher: "Look, we don't believe in reincarnation the way you do. There is only one life on earth, one chance, one judgment. Animals have no incarnation; only man is made in the image of God."

Later that day, the teacher told Ralph: "Now I see that our religions really are different."

Even Ralph's best friend, the Tibetan whose home he had visited earlier, has been very slow in coming to an understanding of Christian truth. It was only after two years of friendship that Ralph felt free to begin studying the Bible with him. And now, after four years, Ralph's friend has finally come to a point where he can say, "I have a place in my heart for Jesus." Ralph aches for this friend to come to Christ. And on the day, by God's grace, when his friend says, "I believe," Ralph will know that his faith is true, because his friend knows all too well what it will cost to follow Jesus.

Of the many insights I gained from my interview with Ralph and Rhonda, one important insight concerned the raising of their children. Fear for the children's safety is often used by young couples as an excuse for resisting God's call to the mission field. I say "excuse," because it is never a legitimate reason for disobeying God's call. There is only one "safe" place for our children anyway, and that is in God's will. The best way we can ensure our children's welfare is by obeying God. And Ralph and Rhonda have proved that to be true.

On their first furlough their son Joshua was diagnosed as having Attention Deficit Disorder (ADD). This, of course, has affected his behavior and development. Joshua had trouble both with concentration and with obedience. He seemed to realize that all too often his behavior was "naughty" and that he needed Jesus to help him become a good boy. At age five he placed his faith in Jesus, and Jesus honored that childlike faith. Since that time Joshua has become sensitive and empathetic to a remarkable degree. His heart is open and responsive to those in need. Yes, he still is working through his problems with ADD, but he is learning to cope with it. He is now in a local national school, and is making friends and doing well in a classroom setting. Ralph and Rhonda have no doubt that Joshua is better off growing up in that overseas environment. Having seen Joshua at age seven, I too have no doubt that their assessment is correct. Joshua seemed to me to be a basically happy and well-adjusted child. God has already honored his parents' faithfulness and obedience. Ralph and Rhonda's experience confirms my own long-held belief that it's better on average to raise children on the mission field than in North America.

Toward the end of our interview together, Ralph told me about a relief agency that had recently provided five hundred yaks for a particularly impoverished area inhabited mainly by Tibetans. Some time later Ralph was able to visit one of the men who had received a yak. Ralph asked him, "Do you have hope now?"

The man went into his hut and came out with a *mani* stone on which some Tibetan words were engraved. "This is my hope," he said.

Paul's second epistle to the Corinthians came to Ralph's mind, in which Paul says that our "letter" is written "not on tablets of stone but on tablets of human hearts" (2 Cor. 3:3). Ralph and Rhonda have given their lives to writing their letter, not on stones, but on the hearts of the Tibetan people.

TROPHIES OF GOD'S GRACE

CHAPTER SEVENTEEN

In Ralph and Rhonda's city there are a dozen other volunteers, some teaching English, some learning one of the national languages, some doing both. Most are couples. I thought to myself that it must be hard to work here as a single person. The Tibetans are so difficult to get to know; it often takes years to make genuine friendships with them. A single person would likely struggle with loneliness in a place like this.

I wish I had space to write about all the volunteers working here and elsewhere, whom I have met in the course of my travels. Each one has a fascinating tale to tell of God's leading and God's grace. In this same city not far from Ralph and Rhonda's university, there is a second university where I met another couple: Barry, an African-American, and his wife Claire, a lovely Anglo-Saxon from New Zealand. The story about how they were led to work among Tibetans and then joined together as husband and wife is a story of God's faithfulness and watchfulness over every detail of their lives.

Barry and Claire had each individually been called to work among Tibetans, and they met for the first time in Lhasa. As their friendship grew, each repeatedly asked God for a sign that they were meant for each other, and God step by step gave those signs. Much of their courtship was through correspondence. At one point Claire, who was in Lhasa, wrote to Barry about the trouble the "Ed. Bureau" (Education Bureau) was causing her. Barry thought some guy named Ed Bureau was after her, and so his next letter was written with unaccustomed warmth and not a little jealousy. This was the letter Claire had been waiting for to prove Barry's seriousness. They got married in Hong Kong, and had now ended up in Ralph and Rhonda's city.

The opportunity I had to meet with a number of workers in that city reinforced in my mind several important truths about such ministry. First, the unity and mutual love these workers manifested toward each other was in itself a strong testimony to the love of God and His power to change people's lives. The nationals noticed how these foreigners were considerate of one another, forgave one another, and sacrificed for one another. They exemplified Jesus' words: "Love one another. . . . By this all men will know that you are my disciples, if you love one another" (John 13:34-35).

The second truth the team exemplified was the necessity of spiritual fellowship. Even though each of the foreign workers in the city had his or her own job responsibility, still on a spiritual level they were one team, one family. One cannot last for long in such circumstances without the encouragement and sustenance that come from being in community with others of like faith. It's warfare out there. Some of the workers told me of the anguishing spiritual battles they had been through. The support they drew from their fellow workers helped them through many of those battles.

A third and related truth that the team exemplified was the need for spiritual boldness. Part of that boldness comes directly from the Holy Spirit. But part is mediated through the community of fellow workers. Work among Tibetan Buddhists is no place for the fainthearted. Hudson Taylor has said: "Winning a Tibetan Buddhist to the Lord is like going into a lion's den and taking a cub." In spite of the spiritual struggles they themselves have endured, Barry and Claire feel that they as a team are on the verge of a breakthrough. "Now is not the time for discouragement," Barry told me. "We have found that praise is a mighty weapon in this warfare. We must not be intimidated, but rather be bold in our witness. The devil would like to paralyze us, inhibit us. Together, and with God's help, we must overcome our timidity and fear. And one of the mightiest weapons we have for doing so is praise. Everyday we concentrate on praising God. This is His battle; it will be His victory."

After a couple of days of meeting workers like Barry and Claire, I found myself thinking that to work in such a place one needed to have the highest possible qualifications, both professionally and spiritually. We needed "only the best" to undertake such work—spiritual giants. "If you're not a Hudson Taylor, you need not apply." And then I met Bill and Jennie Crounse.

I'm not against qualifications, mind you; but sometimes our ideas about qualifications are different from God's. I have heard many young Christians say, "I'm not qualified to be a foreign worker; I don't have this, or I don't have that." And more often than not, I sense they are using their "lack of qualifications" as an excuse for not obeying God.

Take Bill and Jennie. The agency Jennie applied to for going overseas turned her down as unsuited for such service. I recall that Gladys Aylward got turned down too. And Bill had an inauspicious start when he achieved a score of fifteen out of a hundred on a language aptitude test; the passing grade was sixty. He could easily have concluded that he was unsuited for such work. Today he is the world's best nonnative speaker of one of the two primary Tibetan dialects. Meet Bill and Jennie Crounse.

Bill was a commercial fisherman in the Bering Sea. Raised a Roman Catholic, he had experienced a number of close calls at sea, and had become convinced that God was protecting him for some purpose. During that period Bill came to know Christ as his Savior. A short time later he read a biography of Hudson Taylor, and after reading it he felt God calling him to service in Asia. Bill was inspired by Taylor's relationship with God, and he wanted that relationship for himself.

In 1987 Bill enrolled in Prairie Bible Institute in Alberta, Canada, to prepare for his ministry overseas. There he met Jennie Compton. The next year Bill went on a summer trip to Tibet, and sensed God's call specifically to Tibetans. There were very few laborers working among them, and Bill, like the Apostle Paul, wanted to go to an area where no foundation had yet been laid. Two years later, Bill led another summer trip, this time to an area where a different dialect of Tibetan was spoken, and on this trip Jennie went along too. Since there were even fewer laborers working among these particular Tibetans, Bill felt that they were the people he should serve. So after his study at Prairie Bible Institute was finished, Bill made plans to go to Ralph and Rhonda's city in Central Asia and learn this Tibetan dialect.

During their years at Prairie, Bill and Jennie had maintained a casual friendship. Occasionally they would go out to eat, and Jennie recalls that on such occasions she would usually order only soup, and then when Bill offered to pay the tab she'd regret not having ordered a full meal. Jennie did not initially share Bill's calling to Tibetans, but she did have a sense from God that it would please Him if she were to become the wife of an overseas worker. She was willing for that—though she didn't really think Bill would turn out to be that worker!

Jennie had had an exceptionally circuitous route to Prairie Bible Institute. As one of her teammates in Central Asia told me, "Jennie is a trophy of God's grace." Her parents divorced when she was a child. She was sexually abused by both her father and her stepfather. In her early teens she began drinking liquor stolen from her parents. At fourteen she planned to run away from home. But just before she could execute this plan, she was struck down by a drunk driver, and suffered a cerebral contusion that left her unconscious for ten days. When she regained consciousness, her left side was paralyzed and she couldn't speak. She thought to herself, "If this is what my life is going to be like, then I don't want to live."

Jennie is convinced that God healed her supernaturally. Contusions so severe rarely lead to full recovery. But recover she did. Slowly she began to walk and talk again. And as she recovered, she gradually became aware that it was God who was healing her. She had attended Sunday school sporadically as a child, and so had some knowledge of the Bible. But as her recovery neared completion, that childhood knowledge blossomed into faith, and she gave her life to Christ.

Her mother and stepfather had no sympathy with her newfound faith, and opposed her going to church. Her older brother had been kicked out of the house; one younger brother had run away from home, and the other had begun selling marijuana. Yet in spite of her adverse family circumstances, Jennie held on to her faith. She knew Jesus had healed her, loved her, given her new life. She did not want to lose the only thing she had to live for.

Through high school Jennie's faith continued to grow. Then she went to Seattle Pacific University to study nursing, and there she became disillusioned. Her supposedly Christian classmates did not take their faith seriously. She felt that the Christianity she encountered at university was only nominal, cultural. She wanted a faith that was real and true.

She soon developed a relationship with a man who she supposed to be a Christian. However, not long after they began dating, he raped her. For Jennie the experience was devastating. This was someone she had trusted, and he had betrayed and violated her. She went to her closest girlfriend, a Christian, for support and solace; but the girlfriend only said to her: "There must be some sin in your life, and this is the punishment for it."

The words of her friend hurt Jennie deeply. In her distress she called her father. Her father said to her: "Forgive that man; he's no different from me. Just forgive him."

She then called her mother, but her mother's house had only a few days earlier burned to the ground, and the mother had no time for her daughter's problems.

Finally Jennie called a secular rape counseling agency, and they did give her the support she sought. Having found no support from her family and her best Christian friend, she found it in the end from non-Christians. And she began to harden her heart against the church. Soon she stopped associating with Christians altogether.

Even though Jennie still knew Jesus had healed her, that assurance by itself was not sufficient to ground her faith. All these years her faith had been largely emotional and had not been grounded in God's Word. And when negative experiences came, her faith could not sustain her.

Jennie entered a long period of despair and depression. But through it all, she managed to finish her nursing degree. She also took a course in martial arts, hoping to prepare herself for the day when she again might have to defend herself against a man.

In 1987, the same year Bill entered Prairie Bible Institute, Jennie became suicidal. She smashed a mirror in her apartment with the intent to cut her wrists with the broken glass. She felt that demonic forces were pushing her to do it. But before she could injure herself, she became afraid, and called a male friend she had met during her martial arts classes. He was able to calm her.

This friend was a Christian, and he introduced Jennie to a church fellowship that was spiritually alive. Jennie once again began to seek God and call out to Him for help. The first sermon Jennie heard at that church was about being cleansed by the blood of Christ. Jennie thought, "How can blood clean anything?"—a nurse's viewpoint! But then she realized it was true: Jesus' blood does cleanse us. And she wanted that cleansing.

Jennie was not your typical churchgoer at the time. She was accustomed to wearing tight jeans and a leather jacket. She was in the process of buying a motorcycle. She had two boyfriends. But in the midst of her inner desperation, she called out to God: "Show me from your Word what I need to do."

And God opened His Word to her. She read 2 Peter 1:4: ". . . he has given us his very great and precious promises, so that through them you may participate in the divine nature and escape the corruption in the world caused by evil desires." Jennie saw that if she wanted to partake of the divine nature she needed to separate herself from the lusts and corruption of the world. She realized that God was both true and real and that He wanted her whole being, not just part of it. So she said to God, "I'll give you all."

Jennie began to take a greater and greater part in the ministry of her friend's church. She became very close to one of the church members, a woman who like herself had been down in the dregs—a hippie, on drugs, leading an ungodly life. Jennie could identify with this woman. The woman said to Jennie that she ought to go to Prairie Bible Institute. So Jennie applied, and to her amazement, they accepted her.

Jennie's time at Prairie was deeply healing. In her words: "My pride and selfishness were broken. It was a hard time, but also a good time."

It was a good time in another way too: it netted her a husband. But that didn't happen automatically. In fact, Jennie didn't think it would happen at all.

Following their summer trip together to Central Asia in 1990, Bill began to take more notice of Jennie as a potential mate. But Bill was worried lest a wife impede his fulfilling of God's will for him. He did not want to become entangled. Furthermore, as far as he knew, Jennie felt no call to work among Tibetans. So Bill decided that he would actually leave for Central Asia without talking seriously with Jennie about marriage; that way, there was no chance that he would become entrapped.

En route to Asia, Bill had to change planes in Los Angeles. He decided to call Jennie from the airport there to say good-bye. He asked her over the phone: "Are you willing to have a long-distance relationship with me?"

"What do you mean by that?" she asked.

He hemmed and hawed.

She said, "Are you trying to say you love me?"

"Yes!" he said.

Four months after Bill got to Ralph and Rhonda's city in Central Asia, he wrote a prayer letter to his friends and supporters saying, among other things, that he now had a girlfriend. In his next prayer letter four months later he wrote that he had gotten engaged. And in his next prayer letter four months after that, he announced that he had gotten married! For after Bill had been one year in Central Asia studying Tibetan, he had gone back home and married Jennie.

During that first year in Central Asia before his marriage, Bill experienced in a profound way the power of prayer in spiritual warfare. He had been invited by his language teacher to attend the Water God Festival, a vestige of the ancient Tibetan Bon religion, which was held annually in his teacher's village. At various points during the four-day festival, a medium takes on the spirit of the water god and allows himself to be possessed by the water demon. The men of the area gather around and cheer the medium on; then, once possessed, the medium dances and utters oracles. All this is thought to ensure that the next harvest will be a good one.

As Bill observed the festival and talked to his language teacher about it, he experienced a spirit of fear taking hold of him. Then on the third day of the festival, as the medium was beginning to take on the water god's spirit, Bill started to pray. In particular he began to praise Jesus, calling Him the Lord of lords and the King of kings. Bill prayed: "I say in Jesus' name that the devil has no authority in this place." While Bill prayed in this manner, the medium continued his attempt to become possessed by the water demon; but he could not. Finally he collapsed in exhaustion.

Bill realized that it was God's Spirit who had overcome the water god's spirit. Bill had been all alone, afraid and helpless; but before his eyes the Holy Spirit had overcome the devil's power in that place. The memory of that experience has been an encouragement to Bill ever since.

Three years later, with his wife Jennie and a Tibetan Christian friend, Bill returned to the village for the Water God Festival. Prior to the festival, Bill had taught English there, and Jennie, using her nursing skills, had treated many sick people. In the middle of the festival Bill and Jennie were invited to come to the temple in the village to receive recognition and thanks for their service to the community. They were given seats of honor at the entrance to the temple. The village leaders presented them with ceremonial scarves, a traditional token of appreciation in Buddhist cultures. At that very moment, right in front of the temple where Bill and Jennie and their Christian friend were sitting, the medium of the village went into a trance and started to shake in an effort to take on the water god's spirit. The three believers held each other's hands and began to pray in Jesus' name. The medium tried and tried, and shook and shook, but he could not take on the water god's spirit. Finally he collapsed, exhausted.

The next day the medium brought his wife to Jennie and asked her to examine her knees. While Jennie was examining the medium's wife, Bill asked him, "How did you become the medium of this village?"

The man answered, "I was selected by the village elders. But I don't like my work. What I do is not good; what you do is good. You have true compassion; that is the difference between your way and our way."

Bill and Jennie had been in Central Asia together for four years when I met them. Jennie has had many opportunities to use her nursing training to demonstrate Jesus' compassion for the sick. On a number of occasions she has witnessed supernatural healings in response to prayer. Though she still feels her primary calling is to be Bill's wife, she has now gained through the Holy Spirit her own love for the Tibetans, a second calling. Bill and Jennie work together as a team: she ministers to people's physical needs, and Bill shares the gospel with them. They have a beautiful and balanced ministry together.

One great sorrow has marred Bill and Jennie's past year: the death of their infant son in September, 1996. Well into her pregnancy Jennie had to make an arduous motor journey on a strategic ministry under-taking, and the following day she noticed some vaginal bleeding. After that things seemed all right, and at eight months the couple returned to Seattle, as planned, to have the baby.

But Jennie had a nagging anxiety that something was going to go wrong, that she would end up returning to Central Asia without a child. She remembered the line from Job 1:21: "The Lord gave and the Lord has taken away; may the name of the Lord be praised." That verse helped her cast her anxiety upon the Lord. Looking back, Jennie feels that the Holy Spirit was preparing her for what was about to happen.

Everything seemed fine in Seattle, except that the baby was a few days overdue. But then one night, with no warning, the fetal heart stopped beating. The doctors never satisfactorily determined the cause of death, but one factor that likely played a role was the hardship of mission life during Jennie's pregnancy—possibly even that motor journey Jennie had taken earlier over the rough roads of Central Asia. She and Bill felt that their child's death was in part a result of their obedience to God, and that God would somehow be honored through that death.

This is not something modern Christians like to hear; we like to think our obedience will lead to happiness, not sorrow. But Bill and Jennie can testify that obedience is costly. It was costly for Jesus; it will be costly for us as well.

Bill and Jennie do not describe their child's death as a blessing. But in some major ways, other blessings have begun to come. They have experienced greater love for each other. Their trust in God has been strengthened, not shaken. They feel more equipped for the spiritual warfare that lies ahead of them. They feel they are more ready now to persevere. A verse that has come to mean much to them is Galatians 6:9: "Let us not become weary in doing good, for at the proper time we will reap a harvest if we do not give up."

And has their child's death actually brought honor to God, which was their hope? Bill and Jennie would answer yes. Bill said to me, as we sat together in their small apartment in Central Asia, "Our child, without so much as taking a breath, has already drawn five people to Christ: my mother, my stepmother, my two sisters and the boyfriend of one of them. They all openly accepted Christ during our child's memorial service. We had faith that out of our child's death somehow life would come, and it has happened."

"I tell you the truth, unless a kernel of wheat falls to the ground and dies, it remains only a single seed. But if it dies, it produces many seeds" (John 12:24).

A SOWER WENT FORTH TO SOW

CHAPTER EIGHTEEN

Some workers labor in one field most of their lives; others are appointed by God to labor in many fields. Elaine Thompson is one of the latter. She has spent twenty-five years of her life laboring in one field after another—starting in western Nepal, then eastern Nepal, then on to a neighboring country, then further on to the eastern edge of the Central Asian plateau, and finally on to this city in the far north where the high plateau land meets the Gobi Desert. It was in this city—not far from where Ralph and Rhonda lived—that I finally caught up with Elaine. She agreed to meet with me in a public park; this was safer than meeting in her apartment, and would raise less questions.

I had known Elaine during our early years in Nepal together. But I hadn't seen her in a long time. When she came to my hotel to fetch me, I thought to myself, "She hasn't changed much since I saw her last—maybe a little plumper, but as good-looking as ever." She still had the same impish, bouncy air that I remembered, and her brown eyes twinkled with humor as before. I recalled how in Nepal Elaine would periodically enliven our team meetings with tales of her latest exploits, and leave us nearly rolling off our chairs with laughter. She was a valuable corrective to those of us who took ourselves too seriously.

"Come on, *daaju* (older brother)," she said to me. "I know where we can go and talk without being disturbed." I followed her, and in several minutes we came to a small, out-of-the-way park, where we found a low cement wall to sit on.

When I first met Elaine in Nepal in the early 1970s, she was a twenty-two-year-old science teacher working with a volunteer organization. She had just trekked up the mountain to our mission hospital bringing with her a patient from her village. She was a petite and pretty brunette, and I remember being amazed that she should be living all alone down in a Nepali village at the base of our mountain. This girl had gumption.

After we had settled ourselves and eaten a snack Elaine had brought, she began to fill me in on how God had first led her to Nepal. She was already a Christian, she told me, and she had just graduated from college and was looking for a job in the U.S. as a science teacher, but there were no openings. Among the many applications she filled out, one was for a secular volunteer organization that worked in developing countries. It turned out that this organization had an opening for a science teacher in Nepal. Nepal had not been on Elaine's list of countries she might have chosen to work in; the only thing she knew about Nepal was that Mount Everest was there. So she quickly read up on Nepal, and decided to apply for the post.

Since Nepal was the hippie drug center of the world in those days, Elaine's organization tried to weed out those who only wanted to be part of the drug scene there. So during a four-day orientation, the people in charge presented a dreadful picture of Nepal—sickness, isolation, rats, leeches, snakes, awful food, no plumbing or electricity, miles of walking—in order to screen out those applicants with inferior motives. Elaine was not deterred.

Her main concern was whether she could learn the language. During the four-day orientation, a brief Nepali language lesson was given, and in half an hour Elaine had learned to say, "My name is Elaine. What is your name?"

"I've learned two sentences in half an hour," Elaine thought to herself. "This language can't be so hard."

And so it turned out. Once she got to Nepal, Elaine learned the language easily. She had one scare though. During her in-country immersion language course, she lived with a Nepali couple who spoke mainly Newari in their home, one of Nepal's many tribal languages. For the first several weeks Elaine thought she was getting nowhere, because she couldn't understand a word her host couple were saying. Only later did she realize they hadn't been speaking Nepali at all, but Newari. Once that confusion had been straightened out Elaine made rapid progress, and by the end of four months she was teaching science in a village school. By the end of a year she was fluent in Nepali.

By the end of a year she was also sick—with dysentery. In addition, she was homesick and discouraged. She wondered if she could stand one more day of the villagers staring at her as if she were some kind of curiosity. She thought to herself: "I'll just chuck this whole volunteer business and go home."

She prayed about it. Then she thought: "It's only one more year. It's not as if I had to spend ten years here. I can live with just one more year."

After Elaine made the decision to stay, her problems no longer seemed so troublesome. Her second year was much more enjoyable than her first. She got used to village life, she made many more friends, and by the time her second year was up she was feeling nostalgic about the place.

But when the villagers asked Elaine to come back and visit them, as they always do, Elaine said, "I'm not planning to come back. Don't look for me." She wanted to be honest with them.

Elaine's organization had strict rules forbidding its volunteers to talk with nationals about religion. But Elaine talked with Nepalis about Jesus. He was a friend, not a religion. Just before she left Nepal she had a chance to visit the leading church in Kathmandu and was greatly impressed by the preaching of the Nepali pastor. She determined thereafter to pray for Nepal and for the Christians there.

When Elaine arrived back in the States she got a job as a science teacher in her hometown, and taught there for two years. She was enjoying herself, but the thought kept nagging at her: "Anyone can teach science in their own hometown; but not anyone can teach in a place like Nepal." And the thought kept coming back to her: "Maybe I should return to Nepal."

It wasn't that Christian school teachers weren't needed in America; they certainly were. But the need for Christian teachers was much, much greater in Nepal; there were so few Christians there. Elaine came to the point where she said to God, "I am willing to go or to stay. If you want me to go to Nepal, you will have to show me how to do it."

Although Elaine had visited our mission hospital a few times, she didn't really know that much about missions. Moreover, she was thinking in terms of a long-term commitment in Nepal—in spite of her difficult volunteer experience. So she decided to put out a fleece: "I am willing to go," she said to God, "but you must show me how."

And God showed her. The very next Sunday at church, a person said to her out of the blue, "Are you thinking about going back to Nepal? If so, you could go with our agency."

"That's odd," thought Elaine. "Why would he say that?"

The following Sunday, Elaine was in another state in a church of another denomination, and a couple she barely knew came up to her and said, "If you are thinking about going back to Nepal, you could go with our agency."

"That was two times in one week," Elaine said to me. "Was God trying to tell me something?"

Then Elaine told me something I had completely forgotten: "And a few days after that second episode, it happened a third time; I got a letter from you, Tom—from Nepal. And you wrote: 'Are you thinking about going back to Nepal? If so, you could go with our agency.'"

Elaine looked me in the eye and said, "That clinched it. My being here today is basically all your fault!"

Elaine said that she wrote to all three of those agencies, but the one that caught her attention was my own. She felt as if God was tapping her on the shoulder, saying, "You could go with them." And in the end, that is what she did.

Elaine started her long-term career in Nepal near the mission hospital where my wife Cynthia and I worked for twelve years. Elaine taught science in the village school nearby. One of the first of her many stories we used to enjoy so much was about a demonstration of centrifugal force that she conducted for her class of sixth graders. She had brought a half-filled bucket of water to class, and in the manner of science teachers, she had told the incredulous students that she was about to raise the bucket upside down over her head and the water would not spill out. Did they believe that was possible? Of course not, they said. Well, just you watch, said the science teacher. And Elaine began to swing the bucket back and forth in a greater and greater arc, and when sufficient momentum had been gained, she swung the bucket up, up, directly above her—where it struck a horizontal beam in the ceiling and promptly emptied its contents on Elaine's head. The class whooped and cheered. It's surely a gifted teacher who can make science so much fun.

After a year with us, Elaine moved to a village called Tatopani, a full day's walk away, where no Christian had ever worked before. There she and a variety of coworkers spent the next seven years teaching in the local high school. We didn't see too much of Elaine during those years, but whenever we did she always had stories to tell.

Sometimes Elaine contributed to our mission-wide newsletter in Nepal. At one point she advertised a cookie-baking contest, of which she would be the judge. Contestants were to send their entries to her in Tatopani (a full box was required, with bonus points for chocolate-chip cookies), and she would select the winner. The grand prize: a week in Tatopani at the winner's expense.

During the course of Elaine's seven years in Tatopani, a small group of Nepali believers began meeting together. But toward the end of her stay, Elaine realized that they had become too dependent on her; thus she felt she ought to move on and let the believers mature on their own. So Elaine left Tatopani and took a teaching assignment out in a remote area of northwestern Nepal called Dolpa.

Dolpa was a major stop on the trading route used by Tibetans to transport goods between India and Tibet. So Elaine became interested in the traders who passed through town with their long mule trains laden with goods, and she began to frequent a Tibetan tea shop that catered to these traders passing through. She engaged the Tibetan proprietress of the tea shop in lengthy religious discussions, in which the relative merits of Hinduism, Buddhism, and Christianity were compared and debated. But the discussion always ended with the proprietress or one of her customers saying: "It's fine for you Westerners to be Christians, but we Tibetans are born Buddhists. The teachings of Christ are wonderful, but we Tibetans have to be Buddhists. Anyway, there is no real difference between Christ and the Buddha; they are the same." Elaine realized that she was not getting through to them. But in spite of her frustration at not being able to communicate with these Tibetans on a spiritual level, Elaine had begun to feel an attraction, indeed a calling, to minister to Tibetan Buddhist people.

After a year in Dolpa, Elaine was offered an important new assignment, this time in eastern Nepal among the Rai people, one of Nepal's most unreached tribes. And being the perpetual pioneer that she was, Elaine accepted this new challenge.

The Rais were primarily animists, with some elements of Buddhism added on. Elaine applied herself to learning the Rai language; her teacher was an eleven-year-old boy. She also taught English in the local high school.

Not far from Elaine's village a Japanese Christian couple was living; they too were ministering among the Rai people. Twice a week Elaine would walk twenty minutes down a steep rocky path to their house for prayer and fellowship, usually in the evening. On the way back it would be dark, and although the trail in some parts was frequented by drunks and in other parts was wild and uninhabited, Elaine was never afraid. Frequently she made the journey without a flashlight; on a moonlit night the rocks would glow and Elaine could almost imagine that they were angels stationed along the way to guard her.

Near the path lived an older woman who sold tangerines and was known as the "tangerine lady." One evening this woman stopped Elaine and asked her, "How can you walk along this path at night and not be afraid of demons?"

"What demons?" asked Elaine.

The woman described a particular section of the path where the demons hung out, and she went on to describe to Elaine how these demons harassed her whenever she passed by that place.

Elaine said to her, "I am a Christian, so I don't need to fear demons. Jesus Christ is with me, and He is more powerful than any demon."

Two days later the tangerine lady stopped Elaine on the path and said to her, "It works."

"What works?"

"Your Jesus. Last night the demons tried to bother me again, but I told them, 'You can't come here, because Jesus is here.' And they stopped bothering me."

Elaine and the Japanese couple later led that woman to Christ, and she was never bothered by demons again.

Not far from Elaine's village lived a Rai woman whose husband, a believer, had recently been put in jail for his faith. Another Rai believer named Kalan came to this woman's house to see how she was getting along, and he offered to plough her fields for her—something her husband would ordinarily have done. The villagers were amazed that this young man would come and plough this woman's fields for nothing—and he wasn't even a relative. When they asked Kalan why he did it, he said it was because he was a Christian.

About that time a teenage girl in the village began acting strangely, and the local witch doctors were called in but were unable to help her. Knowing that this kind young visitor was a follower of Jesus, the girl's parents decided to ask Kalan to see their daughter, hoping that maybe Jesus could help her. Kalan went to their house and saw that the girl was demon-possessed, and so he prayed for her deliverance and she was healed.

The witch doctors were duly impressed and grudgingly acknowledged the power that Kalan had displayed in Jesus' name. But after a few days they reversed themselves, saying it had actually been their own rituals and incantations that had broken the demon's hold on the girl, but that the effect had merely been delayed. Thus it had only appeared to be Kalan's prayer that had delivered the girl.

As soon as the witch doctors' revised version of events began to circulate throughout the village, the girl relapsed and became worse than before. Again the witch doctors used all their arts and power, but by the end of two days the girl had not improved. Kalan was again called, and this time he rebuked the witch doctors. "Do not treat lightly the power of the one true God," he said, "lest a worse fate fall on you than has fallen on this poor girl." Then he prayed, and the girl was again restored to her right mind.

With that the witch doctors repented and believed in Christ. Then they asked Kalan to baptize them, but he replied, "I am only a young man and not ordained. I will go to Kathmandu and send out a pastor who can baptize you."

But some of the older witch doctors protested, saying, "We are old. We might die before that pastor can come. We do not want to face Jesus without having been baptized."

So Kalan baptized the five oldest witch doctors right then and there, and promised to send the pastor to baptize the rest.

Such stories are not rare in Nepal, nor have they been rare in Elaine's experience. In every place she has worked, she has seen the power of the Holy Spirit manifested in bringing men and women to salvation, in delivering them from demonic oppression, and in physically healing their bodies. In one instance she even witnessed a dead child restored to life. Elaine has seen the fulfillment of the prayer recorded in Acts 4:29-30: "Lord ... enable your servants to speak your word with great boldness. Stretch out your hand to heal and perform miraculous signs and wonders through the name of your holy servant Jesus."

During Elaine's time among the Rai people, she discovered two things: first, she was still able to learn a new language quickly; and second, she enjoyed teaching English. Since Elaine knew that in the future there were going to be many more openings for English teachers than for science teachers, she decided to prepare herself to teach English. So on her next furlough in the USA, she took a TESL course. And when she returned to Nepal she accepted an assignment teaching English in the business school that our mission had recently opened in Kathmandu.

While in Kathmandu Elaine boarded with a Tibetan family—one more step in her eventual calling to work among Tibetan (or Lamaistic) Buddhists. She learned much about Tibetan Buddhism living with this family. Once, on the Tibetan New Year, the hostess served a special soup with nine ingredients, and each person's bowl was filled three times. On the third time the dregs left in each one's bowl were poured over a little figure made of dough, and the particles of the soup stuck to the dough. This represented the demons in the house attaching themselves to this figure, called the "dough boy." Then the dough boy was taken outside to a nearby crossroads, and there it was shattered and left at the intersection. By doing this, the family believed they could rid their house of demons and that the demons would take the wrong road and not be able to find their way back to the house.

As each person poured the dregs from his or her bowl onto the dough boy, it came around to Elaine's turn. The hostess said to Elaine, "You're a Christian; you don't believe in this, do you?"

"No," said Elaine.

"Then you don't have to do it."

Elaine thought: "Thank you, Lord, for getting me out of this dilemma."

Elaine learned many other things about Tibetan Buddhist customs and beliefs. One of them she knew already: Tibetan Buddhists believe that killing any living creature is a sin. One day at dinner a mosquito landed on the table next to Elaine, and she smashed it with her hand. As she withdrew her hand, everyone's eyes were fixed on the dead insect. Shamefaced, Elaine looked up and said, "You don't kill mosquitos, do you?"

"No."

"You believe it's a sin, don't you?"

"Yes."

"Well," said Elaine, flicking the dead mosquito onto the floor, "I can't deny it; I am a sinner." And—she wanted to add—Jesus Christ came into the world to save sinners. That was something this family needed to know.

Elaine pointed out that Tibetans have no qualms about spraying DDT in their outhouses, or poisoning stray dogs. Wasn't that killing too?

No, was the answer. Poisoning is different from killing. The one ingesting the poison is taking its own life: there's no sin there. The mosquito flies into the outhouse and, in effect, commits suicide. That was quite acceptable. Elaine reflected that this must be why poisoning was so common among Tibetans as a method of getting rid of one's enemies: it wasn't a sin!

During that year in Kathmandu, Elaine felt increasingly challenged by the lack of laborers in a neighboring closed country. Over a million Lamaistic Buddhists lived in that country, and there were almost no workers among them. As Elaine prayed for workers for this country, she had to ask herself: "Supposing God wanted me to go to there; would I be willing to go?" She struggled with that. She had moved from place to place so many times that she had a strong desire to put down roots in Nepal and stay put. But gradually Elaine came to the point where she could say to God, "I am willing to go to that country."

Then Elaine learned about an opportunity to study that country's language in a university in Central Asia. She thought to herself, "I can go and study that language for two years, and then see what the Lord opens up for me." And so she decided to take the opportunity to study this new language.

One week before she was to leave Nepal, Elaine was struck by a bicycle as she was walking along a street in Kathmandu. The impact knocked her down right in front of an oncoming bus. As she fell to the pavement her glasses flew off, and she vividly remembers thinking, "My glasses will be crushed"—when, in fact, it was her head that was about to be crushed. The bus stopped within inches of where Elaine was lying.

Then the cyclist who had run into Elaine came up to her and demanded she pay for his bent front wheel. Elaine replied that she would be happy to pay his bicycle bill if he would pay her medical bill, whereupon he promptly disappeared.

On Elaine's last night in Kathmandu, the students in the English class she had been teaching threw her a farewell party. As the party was nearing its conclusion, Elaine announced: "I have to go now. I haven't packed yet, and I'm leaving Nepal in the morning."

The spokesman among the students said, "Before you go, we need to give you a toast."

Elaine said, "Okay."

The spokesman then stood up and said, "We have all decided to become Christians."

After a moment of stunned silence, Elaine said, "Why on earth would you want to do that?"

The spokesman said, "You are a Christian; we want to become Christians too."

"Why?" asked Elaine. "Do you know what it means to become a Christian in Nepal? You may go to jail, you will be ostracized, disinherited, kicked out of your village. Why do you want to be Christians?"

One of the students said, "I'm not sure we know why; we just want to be Christians."

Then Elaine told them what it really meant to be a Christian, who Jesus was, why He came. And she repeated what it might cost them to follow Him. Then she left.

The next morning Elaine told the teacher who was replacing her about the students' desire to become Christians. And though Elaine has no direct follow-up, given the current explosion of the church in Nepal it is not unreasonable to suppose that some of those students have indeed become Christians and joined the ranks of the half million believers in that land.

Soon thereafter, Elaine found herself in Central Asia studying the language of the neighboring closed country to which God was calling her. But this language, which she had thought to master within two years, was much more difficult than she had supposed. At the end of the two years she had reached the same level of proficiency in this new language that she had reached in the Nepali language after only four months!

During her two years of language study in Central Asia, Elaine had the chance to go with her teacher on a field trip to a strategic Buddhist city. While there, the teacher took Elaine and his two other students into a sacred temple in the old part of the city. There in the dimly lit interior, Elaine saw many objects of occult religious art, including a large fresco depicting the eleven hells of Lamaistic Buddhism. Each hell was a different level of punishment for different sins: there was a hell of fire, a hell of ice, a hell of boiling oil, a hell of sharp knives. Demons could be seen slicing up people's tongues, tearing their limbs off, disemboweling them. As they were gazing at this fresco, Elaine's teacher said, "Isn't it beautiful!" And then Elaine realized just how spiritually blind he was: this fresco was not beautiful; it was grotesque.

It was not as if Elaine's teacher had never been exposed to the gospel. Many of his former students had been Christians. He had been given a New Testament in his own language. He had even at one point prayed to receive Christ, though he later admitted it hadn't been for real. Elaine herself had witnessed extensively to this man. In some ways he seemed so open, but in other ways he remained closed and resistant.

Elaine said to me, "It takes an average of twelve years for a Lamaistic Buddhist to come to Christ. They have a totally different world-view. They need to have their minds renewed, as Paul says in Romans 12:2. But we must be patient. I am convinced that God has placed His hand on that teacher. Conversion is a process; he is on the way. Workers among Lamaistic Buddhists must be in it for the long haul. As with this teacher, God may use many workers in just one person's life. One plants, another waters, another reaps."

Then Elaine told me something else about her experience inside that sacred temple that day. "I was having a difficult time looking at all the idols and religious artifacts," she said. "I felt a heavy spiritual oppression inside that place. So I looked instead at the people themselves who had come on pilgrimage to this temple. Many had walked for days, periodically prostrating themselves on the ground as they journeyed. And here they had arrived at the heart and center of their religious faith—the mecca of Lamaistic Buddhism—but they did not look happy. They should have been filled with joy. Instead they looked anxious and afraid. They were in bondage."

As Elaine looked at these pilgrims, she realized afresh that these were people whom God loved and for whom Jesus died. And along with that realization came the growing sense that she herself should return to serve full-time in this very city.

As Elaine and her two fellow language students left the dark interior of the temple, they found a stairway leading up two flights to the roof above, where they came out into the bright sunlight and gazed over the beautiful surrounding landscape. Overhead the sky was blue, and great white clouds floated by. The contrast between the inside and the outside could not have been greater. Simultaneously the three of them began to sing out loud: "His name is higher than any other." God was obviously higher; how could anyone not see it?

After Elaine's two years of language study in Central Asia were finished, she went home to the USA for a furlough. Before she left Central Asia, the agency she was with asked her: "What are you thinking to do when you return?"

Elaine blithely replied, "If the university in that strategic Buddhist city I visited offers me a teaching job, I'll take it."

She was half-joking; she knew it was an impossibility. The whole area was hardly open to resident foreigners at the time, and she already knew that her own agency had no openings there. So Elaine was really without a job, without a country. She missed Nepal terribly. It was with many unanswered questions in her mind that Elaine returned to the USA that year for her furlough.

During her time at home, another agency that places volunteers throughout Asia approached Elaine's own agency, asking if they had anyone who could take an English-teaching post in that very city where Elaine wanted to work! Elaine's agency immediately contacted her, and she accepted.

Elaine then spent the next two and a half years teaching English in that city. It was a rich, challenging, trying time. She lived through a local nationalist uprising, provoked when occupying soldiers stationed on the rooftops around the city's main temple got drunk and threw beer bottles down on the pilgrims coming to worship there. It is not possible to recount the details of Elaine's life there during those years. But that many, many seeds were planted I have no doubt.

At the end of Elaine's two and a half years in that city, an international diplomatic incident resulted in the expulsion of all U.S. citizens living there. And so Elaine was forced to relocate to her present city near the Gobi Desert. Here she teaches English to Lamaistic Buddhists and other ethnic groups. And, as always, she makes friends, and through her life she demonstrates Christ's love for the people of Central Asia.

Elaine's major frustration has been that she rarely gets to see the results of the seeds she plants. With the exception of her seven years in the Nepali village of Tatopani, Elaine has moved from place to place on the average of every two years. She has learned to hold relationships lightly, and to pass on to her successors the national friends she has made along the way.

Whenever I hear a worker telling of some national who has recently come to Christ, I think of Elaine. I think of the seeds she has planted—perhaps five or ten or twenty years ago—that only now are coming to fruition. Those who harvest today are harvesting the fruit of another's labor. Elaine exemplifies what Jesus taught in John 4:37-38: "Thus the saying 'One sows and another reaps' is true. I sent you to reap what you have not worked for. Others have done the hard work, and you have reaped the benefits of their labor."

For many years to come workers will be reaping what Elaine Thompson has sown.

IN THE REMOTE HIGHLANDS OF CENTRAL ASIA

CHAPTER NINETEEN

"If you are writing a book on ministry to the Tibetan Buddhist world, you need to talk to Jari Kostamo," the director of a Central Asian volunteer organization said to me.

"Why is that?" I asked.

"Because he is the 'Bruchko' of Central Asia," he replied.

The director was referring to Bruce Olson, the young man who a generation ago had gone off to the jungles of Venezuela and totally immersed himself in the life and culture of the Indians of that region. His book, *Bruchko*, has since become a classic in mission literature, for Olson exemplified a principle that most other workers only talk about: the need to identify with the people one goes to serve. Bruce Olson's story has been an inspiration to thousands of Christians. If there was now a "new Bruce Olson," especially one working among Tibetan Buddhists, I wanted to meet him.

"Where can I find this Jari Kostamo?" I asked the director.

"I'm afraid that won't be easy," the director said. "First of all, there are only two flights a week to his city, and then he lives a three-hour drive farther up into the mountains. He teaches English at the School for Minorities way out in the middle of nowhere."

"He teaches English?" I asked. "His name sounds Finnish."

"Yes, he's a Finn," said the director, "but he teaches English."

I had known quite a few Finns in Nepal, all of whom spoke very passable English, though they often self-deprecatingly called it "Finglish." There was no law, after all, that only native English speakers should teach English.

The director then added, "Even if you get to the school, there's no guarantee he'll be there. He is often off on one or another project. He's been known to suddenly show up here at our office without warning. He is very independent and very hard to pin down. But if you can find him, it will be worth your while. Jari is a unique person. Have you ever heard of anyone else living in a tent during university to save rent money and skiing four miles to class every day?"

It was only much later, as I was planning my trip to visit Ralph and Rhonda and Bill and Jennie, that I realized Jari's city was the same as theirs. Once I got to the city, all I had to do was spend an extra day and drive the three hours out to Jari's school and visit him there.

After my plans had been set and my tickets bought, however, I learned that Jari was in Finland. Well, I thought, so much for meeting him in Central Asia. But on my arrival in Ralph and Rhonda's city, I learned that Jari had just returned from Finland several days earlier. He had gone home for a short time in order to raise money for a new project he was trying to get under way. Not only was he back in Central Asia, I learned, but he had that very day come into the city and I could find him in the same faculty apartment block that Ralph and Rhonda lived in, for that is where he had left his jeep. So on that first evening in the city when I took the Number 2 bus to interview Ralph and Rhonda, I asked them to leave a note on Jari's jeep saying that I was in town and wanted to see him.

I had hardly sat down with Ralph and Rhonda when there was a loud knock on their apartment door, and in walked a tall, strikingly handsome young man with a reddish-golden beard and the manner of one who is always on the run. After greeting the Atkins with whom he was good friends, Jari turned to me and asked, "Is it you who is wanting to see me?"

I said yes, and explained to him my purpose in coming to see him.

"Well, I don't know when I'll have time," he said to me. "I'm driving back to the school tonight. I suppose you could come out there to see me, and I might be able to fit you in between classes. If you can spend a whole day at the school, I can probably give you a couple of hours total—if my students don't interrupt us too often."

I said that would be fine and we settled on my coming out to the school on my last free day in the city. With that he got up, shook hands, and was out the door.

I decided to hire a car rather than risk the uncertainties of local bus transport. I had directions to the school. It was near the edge of an unusual dry lake, and most foreigners hiring cars wanted to go to the lake. When I explained to the person in charge of the car agency that it was not the lake I was wanting to see but a foreign teacher in the School for Minorities nearby, she said, "Oh, you mean the Finn?"

"Yes, that's the one," I said.

"Fine. He is very famous. I have seen him on television."

She went on to tell me that Jari was highly respected in the whole district for having cast his lot with the underprivileged minority peoples, for living alongside them, and teaching them in the school that the government had constructed for them. The Tibetans of the region had recently suffered through a very harsh winter, and Jari had openly publicized their needs and sought help for them—even on television. "He really cares about the people," the woman said. "That's why we respect him."

Jari, I could see, was respected not only by the Tibetans he had come to serve but by the majority people as well. He was proving yet again that the best way to win people's trust is through acts of genuine love. Added to this was the self-sacrifice involved in living in that remote and difficult region. In the people's minds, anyone—especially a Westerner—who was willing to live out there at that school the year round must love the people very deeply. Furthermore, Jari has won the confidence of government officials. He has paved the way for other like-minded volunteers to come and join him. And Jari has accomplished all this in just three short years.

The day selected for my visit to Jari's school turned out to be clear and sunny. It was mid-April. The highway gradually climbed from 7,500 feet to an elevation of over 11,000 feet. The city itself was located partway up the ascent to the Central Asian plateau, and the journey to the school took me the rest of the way to the top. After winding upward along a river gorge, the road finally reached a pass, which was marked by scores of Tibetan prayer flags fluttering in the breeze, and beyond which the whole of Central Asia, it seemed, stretched out before the eye, a land of sweeping plains interspersed with treeless mountains—hundreds and hundreds of miles of bleak yet starkly beautiful landscape. It was over such land that Marco Polo traveled centuries ago. It was over such land that the Mongol hordes rode to conquest and to slaughter. And it is on such land today that Tibetans still graze their livestock and eke out a subsistence living from the cold, dry soil.

As my driver and I approached the school, the dry lake bed came into view. It was only twenty miles across, but on that day a faint haze rose from the sandy flats and prevented us from seeing the far side. We then took a left turn up a dirt road, and in the distance I could see Jari's school, a series of low buildings inside a walled compound. As we drove into the compound, thirty or so Tibetan children were playing on a dirt playground.

The school, at 10,800 feet, was situated on a gentle slope that rose gradually from the lake bed to a group of 13,000-foot mountains overlooking the school. Small, mud-walled compounds dotted the landscape, within each of which was a small Tibetan house, smoke rising from its roof. On the skyline one could see herds of yaks or sheep being tended by Tibetan youngsters. Above the school sat a Buddhist monastery, newly painted.

Jari came out to greet me. After introducing me to a few of the teachers, he took me into his own room, which was at one end of a row of classrooms facing the playground. Jari's room was Spartan by any standard. At the back was a wooden bed, and along one side was a small desk and some cupboards. Near the doorway was a "kitchen" of sorts, with a counter and a basin for washing dishes. Water came from a pump outside. The most essential item in the room was a cast-iron stove with two burners on top. Even in mid-April the room was frigid, and I came to appreciate the stove more and more as the day wore on. It was a wood-burning stove, but in that treeless area there was no wood; so for fuel, dried yak dung was used, which Jari assured me burned hotter than coal, albeit more quickly. Every half hour or so, Jari would go out and fetch another basket of yak-dung "brickettes," and feed them sparingly to the fire.

I could see why Jari had become so well-known and well-liked. First of all, his very appearance stood out. He was a head taller than any other adult around; Asians tend to be on the short side anyway. He had blond hair, whereas everyone else's hair was black. He had strong, northern European features, resembling pictures one sees of Vikings or ancient kings. His sunburnt face was framed by a full golden beard, and his eyes were blue and penetrating. And yet there was also a tenderness in his manner and expression. This was especially noticeable in his easy relations with the schoolchildren. He seemed always to be surrounded by Tibetan youngsters; one would be asking to have a pencil sharpened, another would need some paper, another would have yet some other request. None showed the slightest hesitation about approaching this blond giant from Finland.

Jari first had a class to teach before he could see me. So I sat on a stool in the sunshine outside the open classroom door and watched Jari inside teach English to a roomful of colorfully though raggedly dressed Tibetan youngsters. Jari's own English pronunciation was nearly perfect. He used a video, which he had proudly obtained for the school, and which the kids obviously relished. When the class was over, the children were dismissed for recess, and Jari and I went into his room to talk.

Jari told me he had been "born a Christian." I probably raised my cyebrows involuntarily, for he quickly went on to explain what he meant. His father had been a minister in a Lutheran church, which taught that children of believing parents were born into God's family through baptism. However, as Jari grew older, he found that this "family of God," the church, was not spiritually alive. There was no youth group. His sister was the only real Christian he knew of in the school they went to.

Jari's family lived in a rugged hilly area of Finland; they were outdoor people. When Jari was seven, his father was caught by a sudden change of weather while out walking in the hills, and he lost his way and froze to death. Jari remembers feeling that "it was God's hand." Some time later his mother remarried.

As Jari entered his teen years, his spirit became more and more adventurous and independent. He was fascinated by geography. He learned how the American Indians had been treated by his European forebears, and he told me that if he had been born a century earlier he would have sided with the Indians against the Americans. During his teen years civil war was raging in Ethiopia, and he remembers wanting to join the Eritrean side against the Ethiopians, because the Eritreans did good works such as building schools and orphanages.

Gradually, however, Jari's enthusiasm for championing the downtrodden by military force was redirected into more peaceful channels. In his late teens, he began to read the Bible seriously. And as he read it, he came to believe what it said. It was that simple. Jesus said: ". . . go and make disciples of all nations." If Jesus is God, Jari reasoned, then it is not ours to choose what we want to do or not do—it is ours to do, to obey. It is not a question of whether to go, but where to go.

So Jari determined to go somewhere in obedience to Jesus' Great Commission. Because of his earlier attraction to American Indians and to their life style, Jari at first thought of going to Latin America. The wide-open spaces, the tents, the horses—all these things appealed to him. He decided to go to the USA and enroll in a university and study Spanish. However, he failed the TOEFL exam, which all foreign students must pass to enter an American university, and so he could not carry out his plan.

That summer he attended a Christian camp meeting in Finland, and there he saw a map of the world depicting the various regions according to how reached they were with the gospel. White areas on the map were completely unreached; yellow areas on the map were slightly reached; red areas were mostly reached. There in the center of Asia was a huge, uninterrupted area of white extending from the Himalayas all the way to Siberia. And in the heart of that white area was Tibet.

Jari had earlier read a biography of the famous Indian evangelist, Sadhu Sundar Singh. He recalled the journeys that Sundar Singh had made into Tibet and the hardships he had endured there. Jari also knew that the Tibetans were similar in many ways to the American Indians. As he looked at that map, he felt drawn toward Tibet.

Furthermore, as Jari studied the map he began to see that God's priority was to reach those who were unreached. Jesus said that all nations were to be discipled. Jari remembered Paul's words in Romans 15:20: "It has always been my ambition to preach the gospel where Christ was not known." This was Jari's call to the unreached. He had to give food first to the starving; only then could he give food to those who were already fed. Jari decided he would go to Tibet.

That fall Jari entered university in Finland. Over the ensuing year, his call was strengthened. But he became more and more impatient with the long period of study that seemed to be required in this modern day to prepare workers for the Lord's service. Jari felt it was more important to act than to merely study. The way to maturity in Christ was not through studying but by living, by obeying. He wanted to go out and preach. After all, Jesus picked people with little education to be His disciples. The main thing was to have a heart for God, a heart for people.

Perhaps feeling sensitive that I had spent ten years studying to be a surgeon, I asked Jari, "What about those who are called to be doctors and nurses and engineers? They need a longer time of preparation."

"Yes, yes," Jari said. "Technical knowledge is good, of course. But I need to consider what is the best thing I can give to the Tibetans. Above all, they need Christ. But they have physical needs too. I thought about getting some extra technical skills, even studying medicine. But then I thought it would be better to trust God to heal people rather than become a doctor myself. I have a few skills—mechanics, building, teaching English. I don't have time to handle the present opportunities that are coming to me let alone think about learning new skills."

Jari told me that during his university years he made two trips to northern India, where the greatest concentration of Tibetan refugees was located. By this time he knew beyond doubt that God was calling him to serve Tibetans. It wasn't that he heard an actual voice saying, "Go to Tibetans." Rather, he felt an inner drive compelling him to go.

Jari first thought he would go to western Tibet, crossing over from Ladakh in northern India. On his second trip to the Ladakh area, he attempted to trek northward toward Tibet with an eighty-pound pack. One night he slept on the trail at 14,000 feet, but while he slept a blizzard struck; when he awoke in the morning two feet of snow had fallen, and he couldn't go on. Jari took this as a sign from God that Ladakh should not be his base of operations.

In 1991, following his university study, Jari returned to Central Asia, this time far to the north. There he began studying Tibetan. For three years he traveled about the high desert country, learning Tibetan and teaching English. He could only get tourist visas, so he was never able to stay long in one place. He prayed for a more permanent situation, trusting God to open the right door for him. Jari said to me, "If you are sure of God's call, you can also be sure He will enable you to fulfill that call."

In 1994 God rewarded Jari's faith by providing him with a work permit to teach in the School for Minorities, where he has been ever since. Jari's dream has come to pass; there is nothing he would rather do than live among these Tibetan people in this wild and beautiful place. It's hard to hold Jari down. One day he is miles out in the hills tracking down students who didn't show up for the beginning of school. Another day he drives three hours into the city to discuss future projects with government officials. Another day, he is visiting a sick parent of one of his students.

Indeed, after our interview was completed, Jari said to me, "Come with me a short walk to visit the mother of two of my students. Because she is sick, they haven't been able to come to school."

So Jari and I trekked for a mile out across the dry grassland above the lake to a small, mud-walled compound, where inside the small living quarters a pallid-looking Tibetan woman was making flat crispy bread. She was breathing more heavily than her exertions warranted, and her ankles were slightly swollen. She was in mild heart failure. As with so many patients I had seen in Nepal, this woman's economic circumstances made it nearly impossible to provide her with the treatment she needed. I could see Jari's compassion for this family, and his distress when I told him the outlook was poor. We talked at length with the family and then we prayed for them. As we walked away, Jari said he was determined to do all that he could to help them.

One of Jari's current projects is to establish a children's center several days' journey by dirt road out in one of the remotest and poorest areas of Central Asia, an area that had been particularly devastated by the cruel winter of 1996. The people there have lost almost all their livestock, and they have no other means of livelihood. Jari's vision is to establish a community development program, which will include education, health, vocational training, and care for orphans and desperately poor families. The reason Jari was in the city the day I arrived was to meet with government officials concerning this project.

Jari's independent, pioneer spirit is a gift from God. We need more workers like him. Yes, Jari doesn't fit neatly into our organizational categories, he is not bound by convention, and likely he would not be the best team player. However, if he were other than who he is, he wouldn't be able to do the things he is doing. It takes a special character to live joyfully and productively in such harsh and difficult circumstances. Jari is such a character.

Before I left to drive back to the city, Jari told me about his recent trip home to Finland. He said he was distressed by the state of the church in Europe. "People read the Bible," he said, "but they don't apply it. They have become like the Pharisees, following the outward form of religion but denying its power.

"The faith I see at home is a dead faith," Jari went on. "The Bible says, '. . . faith without deeds is dead.' Jesus says, 'Go, sell everything you have and give to the poor. . . . Then come, follow me.' People don't want to hear that today. Remember how Jesus said, '. . . when the Son of man comes, will he find faith on the earth?' I'm afraid He won't.

"I met with some college students in a church youth group when I was home, and I asked them right out: 'If Jesus showed up here and said, "Come, follow me," would you follow Him?' And only one student said he would.

"Jesus' heart is with the poor, the oppressed, the hungry. Read Matthew 25:31-45. That's one of the most important passages in the Bible. Words aren't enough; action is necessary. Love is action. So I am trying to set up this children's center. I go back to Finland and try to raise $120,000 for it, but one church I visit can't help because they are spending $150,000 to build a summer cabin for the church! How are we ever going to get Christians to do Jesus' will and follow His priorities?"

Jari paused for a moment and then said, "I don't mean to be critical; I have a long way to go myself. My main challenge is not raising money, learning Tibetan, teaching these people about God; my main challenge is changing myself—changing myself into someone willing to give to others whatever God has given me. That way I can show these people what God is like—not just tell them. My desire is that they begin to do for others what I, through God's love and grace, am trying to do for them. Then I will know their faith is real. Then I will know that my coming here was not in vain."

I asked Jari, "Do you have a final word for the readers of this book?"

He replied, "Yes, and it's Jesus' word, not mine: 'I tell you the truth, whatever you did for one of the least of these brothers of mine, you did for me.'"

As my car drove out the school gate, I looked back and saw Jari standing in the center of the dirt playground, a tall, blond figure surrounded by thirty clamoring, laughing Tibetan children.

AFTERWORD

I n this book I have focused not on historical figures but rather on individuals of this present generation, most of whom are alive today. There is a simple reason for this. Historical figures are remote from us. Because they lived in a different time and faced situations we will never face, we cannot so easily put ourselves in their shoes and relive their experiences. We elevate them; we idealize them; and we regard their accomplishments as unattainable by ordinary Christians like ourselves. We consider them supermen and superwomen, and hence we do not feel either called or qualified to follow in their steps. We conveniently forget that they were no different then from what we are today. They were no mightier, no more able, no more spiritual than we. Everything they accomplished for God was accomplished only through God's enabling grace. And that grace is equally available to us today. It is being demonstrated in the lives of the people whose stories I have recounted here, people basically no different from any reader of this book. These people, too, are making history. God is enabling them today to carry out the same kind of pioneer mission work that their predecessors carried out. They are a continuation of a fascinating and glorious heritage.

From the first Nestorian Christians who set out for Central Asia in the seventh century, to the Roman Catholic fathers in the fourteenth through the eighteenth centuries, and on to the Protestant missionaries of the nineteenth and twentieth centuries, God has been calling out His people to penetrate the vast, dark, Tibetan Buddhist world. These pioneers endured incredible hardships: many were imprisoned; others were robbed or beaten; still others suffered from various illnesses; and many others lost their lives, either through sickness or through violence.

Of the Protestants who went out to Central Asia, the Moravians were among the first; their work was centered in Ladakh in northern India, often called "Little Tibet." To the east, other pioneers attempted to enter Tibet from the Indian town of Darjeeling. One of the most courageous was a woman, Annie Taylor, who headed the Tibetan Pioneer Mission. Rebuffed repeatedly at the India-Tibet border, she entered China and tried to reach Lhasa from the Chinese side. In 1892 she came to within three days' journey of Lhasa; before that year only three foreigners had ever set foot in the city. But she ultimately failed to reach her goal.

Many others followed Annie in attempting to reach the Tibetans. Some went out under the old China Inland Mission; others went under various Protestant agencies and denominations. Two of the better-known workers of recent times were George Patterson and Geoffrey Bull, both of whom have written and spoken extensively about their experiences.

To the north, similar efforts had been going on over the centuries to evangelize the Mongols. In more recent times, three missionary families (whom we have already noted) set out on a 4,000-mile sled ride to Siberia and Mongolia and paid a tremendous price. Some years later in 1870, James Gilmour, the most famous of the missionaries to Mongolia, set out from London at the age of twenty-seven to pour out the rest of his life serving in that country. In 1893 Frans Larson, nicknamed the "Duke of Mongolia," went out under the Christian and Missionary Alliance. The Boxer Rebellion struck in 1900, during which time scores of missionaries were brutally murdered. Larson led a group of missionaries and their families on a hair-raising, two-month escape across the Gobi Desert into Russia. When the Boxer madness subsided, he returned to Mongolia, where he and a number of others labored until Mongolia was closed in the 1930s by the Japanese invasion of China. Forty years later, Stephen Collins would be the first foreign Christian to enter Mongolia in the postwar era.

The striking thing about these centuries of sacrifice and effort expended to evangelize the Tibetan Buddhists is that they have been singularly unfruitful. The Tibetan Buddhist world, with but few exceptions, has remained largely impervious to the gospel. Periodically God has blessed the labor of an individual worker or a group of missionaries, and a church has sprung up—only to die away within a generation or two. The only five areas in the Tibetan Buddhist world today where significant inroads have been made are among a certain group of Tibetans in Central Asia, among Siberian Buddhists in the Russian Republic of Tuva, among the Tamangs of Nepal, among the Lepchas of Sikkim, and now, more recently, among Mongols in Ulan Bator. Everywhere else, the number of Christians is counted in double digits.

Far from discouraging us, this small yield should challenge us to renew our efforts to reach these resistant people. James Gilmour labored for twenty-one years in Mongolia and saw only two Mongol converts. And yet his example inspired hundreds of other Western Christians to answer God's call to go out to the harvest fields of Central Asia.

Some Christians say we should concentrate our mission efforts on those who are receptive. They look at missions from the standpoint of cost-effectiveness; they want the biggest bang for their buck. "Twenty-one years and only two converts to show for it?" they ask. "We shouldn't be putting our effort into places like that."

The problem with that line of thinking is that we do not know God's time for a given people. Furthermore, how does a people become receptive apart from the labor and sacrifice of the initial pioneers? The hardest work of missions is to prepare the soil, remove the rocks, and to plant and water the seed. Picking the fruit is the easy part. Jesus Himself told His disciples they would be harvesting fields where others had done most of the work.

As we look at what God is doing in the world today—especially in this current generation—we cannot fail to see that for nation after nation God's time of harvesting has come like never before. The outpouring of God's Spirit in Latin America, Africa, Northeast India, Burma, Nepal, Indonesia, Korea, China, and the former Soviet Union has been unparalleled in the history of the church. Just a hundred years ago we would have labeled most of these places "unreceptive, resistant." Take the Muslim world, for example; it is said that more Muslims have come to Christ in the past twenty-five years than in all the preceding centuries put together.

Therefore, looking at what God has been doing around the world, it is not unreasonable to conclude that God's time of harvest has also come for the Tibetan Buddhist peoples. In these past fifty years doors have been opening into certain areas of the Tibetan Buddhist world that have never been open before. In other areas doors are reopening that have been shut for generations. And we are now seeing the firstfruits of the harvest in places like Nepal and Mongolia.

However, we need to temper our optimism by asking ourselves why there has been so little fruit among Tibetan Buddhists for so long. Has it only been a question of God's timing, or have mistakes been made or wrong strategies employed? God chooses to work through missionaries, through witnesses; but if they bungle it, God's time for a people could be delayed. In our eagerness to win a harvest among Tibetan Buddhists, we must not neglect the lessons of the past nor repeat the mistakes that an earlier generation of missionaries may have made.

Here are some possible reasons that could explain the lack of fruit among Tibetan Buddhists in the past. To begin with, there probably has been too little emphasis on church planting and the discipling of new believers. Many past missionaries have concentrated almost exclusively on itinerant evangelism, and have failed to establish permanent communities of Christians. In other cases, the gospel was perhaps not presented in a culturally relevant way; some workers may have had an inadequate understanding of the host culture and thus failed to adapt their message to that culture. Perhaps too much effort was spent winning individual converts to Christ, and not enough effort was spent bringing whole families and even communities into the faith. Social and political considerations were surely a major cause of the missionaries' lack of success. Above all, the nature of Tibetan Buddhism itself may not have been fully understood; its fundamental premises are starkly opposed to those of the gospel, and only by utilizing all the spiritual weapons at their disposal can Christians hope to stand against it and to prevail. Would a different approach on the part of the missionaries have resulted in more fruit? We must look at all these areas and devise strategies for the future that will correct any deficiencies of the past.

Regardless of our conclusions about the past, Christ's call to us, as always, is to go and make disciples of all nations and to be His witnesses even to the ends of the earth. More important than any other factor in bringing in the harvest is our obedience—in conjunction with God's timing. The timing is God's; the obedience is ours. If Christians will obey Jesus' call and go out as His witnesses among the Tibetan Buddhist peoples, I believe we will see that God's time for the Tibetan Buddhist world is at hand.